Photo Credits

1TL ©2008 Jupiterimages Corporation 1ML ©2008 Jupiterimages Corporation 1BL ©istockphoto.com/Daniek 1R ©istockphoto.com/Andrei Mihalea 6 ©2008 Jupiterimages Corporation 7 ©2008 Jupiterimages Corporation 8 ©2008 Jupiterimages Corporation 9 ©2008 Jupiterimages Corporation 10 ©2008 Jupiterimages Corporation 11 ©2008 Jupiterimages Corporation 12 ©Dannyphoto80 | Dreamstime.com 13 ©Glenjones | Dreamstime.com 14 ©Apresident | Dreamstime.com 15 ©2008 Jupiterimages Corporation 16 ©2008 Jupiterimages Corporation 17 ©2008 Jupiterimages Corporation 18 ©2008 Jupiterimages Corporation 19 ©2008 Jupiterimages Corporation 21 ©2008 Jupiterimages Corporation 22 ©2008 Jupiterimages Corporation 23T ©istockphoto.com/Nico Smit 23B ©2008 Jupiterimages Corporation 24 ©Clivia | Dreamstime.com 25 ©Dejavues | Dreamstime.com 26 ©2008 Answers in Genesis 27 ©2008 Jupiterimages Corporation 28 ©2008 Jupiterimages Corporation 29 ©2008 Jupiterimages Corporation 31 ©2008 Jupiterimages Corporation 32 ©2008 Jupiterimages Corporation 33 ©2008 Jupiterimages Corporation 35T ©istockphoto.com/Johann Helgason 35B ©2008 Jupiterimages Corporation 36 ©2008 Jupiterimages Corporation 37 ©2008 Jupiterimages Corporation 38 ©2008 Jupiterimages Corporation 39 ©2008 Jupiterimages Corporation 40 ©2008 Jupiterimages Corporation 41 ©2008 Jupiterimages Corporation 42 ©2008 Jupiterimages Corporation 43 ©2008 Answers in Genesis 44T ©2008 Jupiterimages Corporation 44B ©2008 Answers in Genesis 45TR ©2008 Jupiterimages Corporation 45M Courtesy Maungatautari Ecological Island Trust 44BL ©Otvalo | Dreamstime.com 46 ©2008 Jupiterimages Corporation 47 ©2008 Answers in Genesis 48 ©2008 Richard Lawrence 49 ©2008 Jupiterimages Corporation 50 ©Carrydream | Dreamstime.com 52 ©2007 John McNeal 53 ©2008 Jupiterimages Corporation 55 ©2008 Jupiterimages Corporation 56 Credit U.S. Fish and Wildlife Service 57 Credit U.S. Fish and Wildlife Service 58 ©2008 Jupiterimages Corporation 59 ©2008 Jupiterimages Corporation 60 ©2008 Jupiterimages Corporation 61 ©2008 Jupiterimages Corporation 62 ©2008 Jupiterimages Corporation 63 ©istockphoto.com/Thomas Mounsey 64 ©2008 Jupiterimages Corporation 66 ©2008 Jupiterimages Corporation 67 ©istockphoto.com/Norma Cornes 68 ©2008 Answers in Genesis 69 ©2008 Answers in Genesis 70 ©2008 Answers in Genesis/Dan Rockafellow 72 ©2008 Jupiterimages Corporation 73 ©2008 Jupiterimages Corporation 75 ©2008 Jupiterimages Corporation 77 ©2008 Jupiterimages Corporation 78 ©2008 Jupiterimages Corporation 79 ©2008 Jupiterimages Corporation 80 ©2008 Jupiterimages Corporation 81 ©2008 Jupiterimages Corporation 81BL ©Prairierattler | Dreamstime.com 83 ©2008 Jupiterimages Corporation 84 ©2008 Jupiterimages Corporation 85 ©2008 Jupiterimages Corporation 86 ©Undy | Dreamstime.com 87 ©Photosaurus | Dreamstime.com 88 ©2008 Jupiterimages Corporation 89 ©Tommyschultz | Dreamstime.com 90 ©2008 Jupiterimages Corporation 91 ©2008 Jupiterimages Corporation 92 ©2008 Jupiterimages Corporation 94 ©Anobis | Dreamstime.com 95 ©2008 Jupiterimages Corporation 96T ©2008 Jupiterimages Corporation 96B ©2008 Answers in Genesis 97 ©2008 Jupiterimages Corporation 98 ©Cathykeifer | Dreamstime.com 99 ©2008 Jupiterimages Corporation 101 ©2008 Jupiterimages Corporation 102 ©2008 Jupiterimages Corporation 103 ©2008 Jupiterimages Corporation 104TL ©2008 Jupiterimages Corporation 104TR ©Kvkirillov | Dreamstime.com 104B ©2008 Jupiterimages Corporation 105 ©2008 Jupiterimages Corporation 106 ©2008 Jupiterimages Corporation 107T ©Jeridu | Dreamstime.com 107B ©2008 Jupiterimages Corporation 109 ©2008 Jupiterimages Corporation 110 ©2008 Jupiterimages Corporation 111 ©2008 Jupiterimages Corporation 112 ©2008 Jupiterimages Corporation 113 ©2008 Jupiterimages Corporation 114T ©2008 Jupiterimages Corporation 114B ©2008 Answers in Genesis 115 ©2008 Jupiterimages Corporation 116 Credit NOAA/U.S. Department of Commerce 117 ©2008 Jupiterimages Corporation 118 ©2008 Jupiterimages Corporation 119 Public domain 120 ©2008 Jupiterimages Corporation 123 ©istockphoto.com/Suzanne Carter-Jackson 124T Public domain 124B Courtesy CDC 125 Credit OAR/National Undersea Research Program 126 ©2008 Answers in Genesis 127 ©2008 Answers in Genesis 128 ©2008 Answers in Genesis 129 ©2008 Answers in Genesis 130 Courtesy CDC/James Gathany 131 Courtesy CDC 132 ©Eraxion | Dreamstime.com 134 Public domain 136 ©2008 Jupiterimages Corporation 138 ©2008 Jupiterimages Corporation

Table of Contents

THE WORLD OF ANIMALS

1:1 answersingenesis
Petersburg, Kentucky, USA

3RD EDITION | UPDATED, EXPANDED & FULL COLOR

God's Design® for Life is a complete life science curriculum for grades 1–8. The books in this series are designed for use in the Christian school and homeschool, and provide easy-to-use lessons that will encourage children to see God's hand in everything around them.

Third edition
Third printing August 2010

ISBN: 1-60092-160-4

Cover design: Brandie Lucas & Diane King
Interior layout: Diane King
Editors: Lori Jaworski, Gary Vaterlaus

Published by Answers in Genesis, 2800 Bullittsburg Church Rd., Petersburg KY 41080

Printed in China

www.answersingenesis.org • www.godsdesignscience.com

WELCOME TO GOD'S DESIGN® FOR LIFE

You are about to start an exciting series of lessons on life science. *God's Design® for Life* consists of three books: *The World of Plants*, *The World of Animals*, and *The Human Body*. Each of these books will give you insight into how God designed and created our world and the things that live in it.

No matter what grade you are in, first through eighth grade, you can use this book.

1st–2nd grade

Read only the "Beginner" section of each lesson, answer the questions at the end of that section, and then do the activity in the box (the worksheets will be provided by your teacher).

3rd–5th grade

Skip the "Beginner" section and read the regular part of the lesson. After you read the lesson, do the activity in the box and test your understanding by answering the questions in the box.

6th–8th grade

Skip the "Beginner" section and read the regular part of the lesson. After you read the lesson, do the activity in the box and test your understanding by answering the questions in the box. Also do the "Challenge" section in the box. This part of the lesson will challenge you to go beyond just elementary knowledge and do more advanced activities and learn additional interesting information.

Everyone should read the Special Features and do the final project. There are also unit quizzes and a final test to take.

Throughout this book you will see special icons like the one to the right. These icons tell you how the information in the lessons fit into the Seven C's of History: Creation, Corruption, Catastrophe, Confusion, Christ, Cross, Consummation. Your teacher will explain these to you.

Let's get started learning about God's design of amazing animals!

UNIT 1

MAMMALS

KEY CONCEPTS

◊ **Distinguish** between vertebrates and invertebrates.

◊ **Identify** the five characteristics of mammals.

◊ **Distinguish** between apes and monkeys.

◊ **Distinguish** between marsupials and other mammals.

UNIT LESSONS

THE WORLD OF ANIMALS

Is it a mouse or a moose?

LESSON 1

What is the difference between vertebrates and invertebrates?

Words to know:

vertebrates

invertebrates

BEGINNERS

Do you like animals? Most people do. Animals are very interesting. They come in all shapes and sizes. Some animals are big such as elephants. Other animals are so small you can only see them with a microscope. Genesis 1 tells us that in the beginning God created various kinds of animals, such as the cat kind, horse kind, and elephant kind. Today, there are many different types of animals within each kind.

Scientists have divided all the animals into two main groups. One group includes all the animals that have backbones. These animals are called **vertebrates**. The other group includes all the animals that do not have backbones. These animals are called **invertebrates**. Most animals that you probably think of are vertebrates. Dogs, cats, horses, birds, and snakes all have backbones.

The vertebrates have been divided into five groups. These groups are mammals, birds, fish, amphibians, and reptiles. We will learn about each of these groups and study some of the wonderful animals in each group.

Later in this book we will also study some of the invertebrates such as jellyfish, insects, spiders, and crabs. We hope you enjoy learning about all the different animals that God made.

- **How many different types of animals are there?**
- **What are the two big groups of animals?**
- **Who made all the different animals?**

Animals and plants are the two largest and most familiar groups of living things. The most distinguishing difference between plants and animals is that plants can make their own food and animals cannot. Animals (and man) were originally created to eat plants to obtain energy (Genesis 1:28–30). Since the Fall of man in the Garden of Eden, many animals still eat plants but others eat animals to obtain energy. Because animals must obtain their own food, they are mobile. They can move about to find plants or animals to eat.

Animals come in all shapes and sizes. Some are so tiny you can only see them with a microscope. Others are as huge as a car or even a house. God originally created various animal kinds, like the cat kind, horse kind, and elephant kind. Since the Flood of Noah's day, these animal kinds have spread around the world and have adapted to different environments, so that today there are many different species of animals within each kind. Scientists have classified over 1 million different species of animals, and there may be millions more that have not been classified.

In order to study so many different types of animals it is convenient to group them together by their similar characteristics. The first grouping that scientists make is to divide animals by whether they have backbones or not. Animals with backbones are called **vertebrates**. Animals without backbones are called **invertebrates**.

The African elephant is the largest living land animal.

Although only 3% of all animals are vertebrates, they are the animals we are most familiar with. Vertebrates are the animals we see around us every day. Every vertebrate has a backbone. The backbone protects the spinal cord that passes through it. Vertebrates have the same major systems that humans have, including skin, skeletal, muscular, nervous, respiratory, and digestive systems. Although all of these systems occur in all vertebrates, they vary considerably among the different kinds of animals.

Vertebrates are divided into five different groups: mammals, birds, fish, amphibians, and reptiles. We will explore each of these groups in more detail.

Invertebrates are animals without spinal cords. They are very diverse and account for nearly 97% of all animals. Invertebrates do not have internal skeletons. Invertebrates include sponges, jellyfish, worms, insects, and many more creatures. We will also study each group of invertebrates in more detail. ■

Squids are some of the largest invertebrates.

Animal Charades

This can be a fun family game. Pretend to be an animal and have everyone else guess what animal you are. Whoever guesses the animal correctly gets to be the next animal. Choose animals other than mammals, with which you are most familiar.

WHAT DID WE LEARN?

- What are the two major divisions of animals?
- What are two similarities among all animals?

TAKING IT FURTHER

- When did God create the different animal kinds?
- How is man different from animals?

Unusual Animals

There are many animals that you are familiar with. But with over a million different species, there are bound to be many that you are unfamiliar with as well. Below is a list of unusual animals. See what you can find out about each of these animals from an animal encyclopedia or other source, and prepare a short report to share with your class or family. Three of them are shown below. Can you identify them?

- Pangolin
- Common snipe
- Echidna
- Grouper
- Liver fluke
- Common whelk
- Queen Alexandra's Birdwing

VERTEBRATES

Does it have a backbone?

LESSON 2

What makes a vertebrate a vertebrate?

Words to know:

vertebrae

BEGINNERS

What do these animals all have in common: a mouse, a lizard, and a goldfish? Even though these animals are very different, they are all vertebrates. Vertebrates have backbones. The backbone protects a spinal cord. Each animal also has a brain that sends messages along its spinal cord to the rest of its body.

Vertebrates also have bones inside their bodies. These bones support the body and allow the animal to move around. A mouse has much smaller bones than an elephant, but they both have bones inside their bodies.

There are five kinds of vertebrates. Mammals are animals that have fur. Birds are animals with feathers. Amphibians are animals that start out breathing water and later change to be able to breathe air. Reptiles are animals that have scales and live on land. And finally, fish are animals that have scales and live in the water. We will learn much more about each of these groups of animals in future lessons.

- **What are two things that all vertebrates have?**
- **What are the five different kinds of vertebrates?**

The animals we are most familiar with are vertebrates. A vertebrate is an animal that has a backbone. The backbone protects the spinal cord that runs inside of it. Vertebrates can be classified into five categories: mammals, birds, fish, amphibians, and reptiles. These are the animals we notice most around us because, in general, they are the largest animals. Although each of these groups of animals has unique characteristics, they have some common characteristics as well.

All vertebrates have spinal cords and brains. These are the major parts of each vertebrate's nervous system. The spinal cord is protected by a backbone, which is really a series of smaller bones called vertebrae, hence the name vertebrates. Messages travel from the animal's brain down the spinal cord to the various parts of the body to tell the animal how to move and what to do. Messages also travel from the various parts of the body along the spinal cord to the animal's brain. Vertebrates have some of the most complex nervous systems of all the animals.

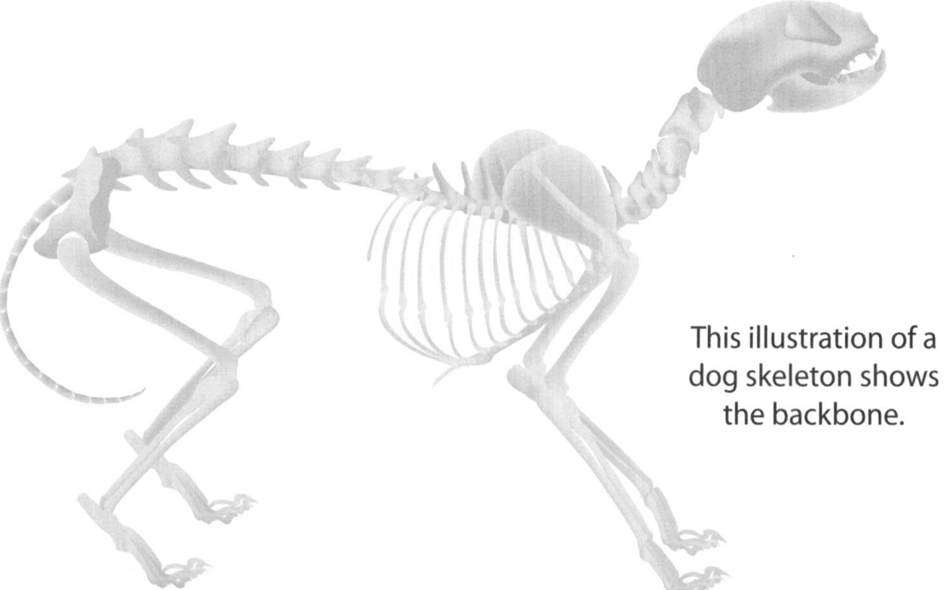

This illustration of a dog skeleton shows the backbone.

Animal Notebook

As you study the world of animals you will be making a notebook that will include your projects. Today, start your notebook by making dividers for each part of the animals we will study. Use the dividers with tabs that are designed for three ring binders. Make labels for each tab in the notebook. Tabs should be labeled as follows: Mammals, Birds, Fish, Amphibians, Reptiles, Arthropods, Mollusks, Cnidarians, Echinoderms, Sponges, Worms, Protists, and Monerans (you may combine Protists and Monerans if you wish).

These are the various parts of the world of animals that you will be studying. Name as many animals in each category above as possible. Some, like mammals, will be very easy, but you may have no idea what animals belong in some of the other categories. As you go through the lessons in the book you can include anything in your notebook that you wish. Some ideas include the projects from this book, photos of projects or activities that you do, photos from field trips, photos cut from magazines, or coloring books and drawings. Use your imagination.

Another common trait that is unique to vertebrates is an internal skeleton. This skeleton is what allows vertebrates to be much larger than most other animals. God gave vertebrates the internal structure needed to support the weight of a large body. Not all vertebrates are large, but nearly all large animals are vertebrates. A few exceptions are the octopus and giant squid. These creatures can be large without an internal skeleton because the water in which they live helps to support their weight. For the most part, vertebrates also have more complex muscular, digestive, and respiratory systems than invertebrates.

We will discuss each group of vertebrates in more detail in the following lessons, but here is a quick overview of the major types of vertebrates. Mammals are vertebrates with hair or fur. They are warm-blooded, and they nurse their young. Birds are warm-blooded animals with feathers. The other vertebrates are all cold-blooded animals. Amphibians are unique because they begin life in the water and as they mature their bodies change and they begin to breathe air through lungs. Reptiles are animals that have scales and breathe air. And fish are aquatic animals that have gills that extract oxygen from the water in which they live. Vertebrates are easy to find and fun to study. Enjoy learning more about God's wonderful creatures. ■

Dogs are mammals; they are warm-blooded and nurse their young.

WHAT DID WE LEARN?

- What are the two major divisions of the animal kingdom?
- What characteristics define an animal as a vertebrate?
- What are the five groups of vertebrates?

TAKING IT FURTHER

- Think about pictures you have seen of dinosaur skeletons. Do you think dinosaurs were vertebrates or invertebrates? Why do you think that?

TITLE PAGE

Use your artistic, computer, and literary skills to create a title page for each section of your animal notebook. If you don't know what kinds of animals belong in some of the sections, look them up in an encyclopedia.

Mammals

The fuzzy creatures

LESSON 3

What makes an animal a mammal?

Words to know:

mammals

mammary glands

warm-blooded

Challenge words:

stance

unguligrade

ungulates

digitigrade

plantigrade

Beginners

Mice and an elephants are both **mammals** because they both have fur. What other animals can you think of that have fur or hair on their bodies? If you said lion, dog, cat, horse, or cow you would be right. And there are hundreds of other mammals as well.

In addition to growing hair, mammals also give birth to babies rather than laying eggs like many other animals. Mammals feed milk to their babies from special parts of their body called **mammary glands.** Some mammal babies nurse for just a few weeks while others nurse for many months before they begin eating other food.

Mammals are **warm-blooded**. This means that their body temperature stays about the same no matter what the temperature is around them. They also breathe air with lungs. When you look at fuzzy kittens, hairy monkeys, or huge elephants, remember that they are all mammals.

- **What are five things that all mammals have in common?**
- **Name three mammals that have not been mentioned in this lesson.**

The most familiar vertebrates on earth are **mammals**. How can you tell if an animal is a mammal? Mammals have five common characteristics. They are warm-blooded, they have hair, they give birth to live young, they feed milk to their young, and they breathe air through lungs. There is great variety among mammals. Some are tiny such mice; others are very large such as the giraffe or the elephant. Most live on land but a few, dolphins and whales for example, live in the water. To identify an animal as a mammal, however, we must examine their similarities.

First, mammals are **warm-blooded**. This means that their bodies stay about the same temperature regardless of the temperature of the air around them. A mammal's body regulates, or controls, its body temperature. To produce heat for the body, mammals must eat a lot of food.

Second, most mammals give birth to live young. Two exceptions are the spiny anteater (echidna) and the platypus, both of which lay eggs. Yet, even these animals feed their young milk from special glands in their bodies. These glands are called **mammary glands**, hence the name mammal. The major deciding factor in an animal being a mammal is whether it nurses its young or not.

Dolphins are not fish; they are mammals.

In addition to these common characteristics, all mammals have hair or fur on their bodies. Some mammals seem completely covered with hair while others have just a little hair. Most hair provides protection from the cold. Hair also helps with the sense of touch. And the color and pattern of hair helps many mammals hide from their enemies.

Finally, mammals breathe air through lungs. Even whales and dolphins have lungs and they must surface periodically to get a breath of fresh air, unlike fish that get oxygen from the water itself through their gills.

After looking at mammal characteristics, you might wonder if humans are mammals. Physically, humans share these same characteristics with mammals, and most scientists would classify humans as mammals. However, we know that man is not an ordinary animal. Man is a spiritual and moral creature who can have a relationship with God. Man alone was created in God's image (Genesis 1:26–27). ■

Mammals Have Fur

Complete the "Mammals Have Fur" worksheet. Use pictures of mammals to describe the fur for animals that you do not have access to. Although people are set apart from animals, compare a sample of your hair to that of some mammals. Add the worksheet to your animal notebook.

WHAT DID WE LEARN?

- What five characteristics are common to all mammals?
- Why do mammals have hair?
- Why is a platypus considered a mammal even though it lays eggs?

TAKING IT FURTHER

- Name some ways that mammals regulate their body temperature.
- What are some animals that have hair that helps them hide from their enemies?

MAMMAL FEET

As you will learn in the following lessons, mammals can be grouped together in many different ways. One way that they can be grouped is by how their feet are designed; this is called the animal's **stance**. The design of an animal's feet determines how that animal will walk. A few mammals, such as whales and dolphins, do not have feet. But most mammals are land dwelling and walk on their feet.

One group of mammals has an **unguligrade** stance and are referred to as **ungulates**. Ungulates walk on the very tips of their toes. This may sound very painful, and for a human this would not be a normal or healthy way to walk. But ungulates have hooves which protect their toes so it is natural for them to walk on the tips of their toes. Horses, sheep, and goats are all ungulates. Animals with an unguligrade stance have extended strides and can often move very fast.

Many other mammals walk on the flats or undersides of their toes. These animals are said to have a **digitigrade** stance. These animals can also move very quickly. The cheetah, considered to be the fastest land animal, has a digitigrade stance. Dogs and cats also fit into this category of mammals.

The third way that mammals walk is with a **plantigrade** stance. These are animals that walk on the soles of their feet. Bears and raccoons have a plantigrade stance. Most animals that walk on their whole foot are not as fast as other animals. The ankle bones and toe bones are very different in the different stances, yet each was designed perfectly for the way each animal moves.

Think about how each of the following mammals walks. Decide which kind of stance that animal has. It might help if you look at pictures of the animals to see how they stand on their feet.

- Deer
- Rabbit
- Giraffe
- Wolf
- Skunk
- Elephant
- Opossum
- Chimpanzee
- Fox

Horses are unguligrade.

Cheetahs are digitigrade.

Raccoons are plantigrade.

Mammals: Large & Small

Armadillo to zebra

Lesson 4

What are the largest land mammals?

Challenge words:

ruminants

rumen

reticulum

cud

omasum

abomasum

Beginners

God has created hundreds of different kinds of mammals. Mammals live in nearly every part of the world, so you have certainly seen many of them. Today we will learn a little about some of the more interesting mammals.

Three of the largest land mammals are the elephant, the giraffe, and the bear. Elephants are very large and have long trunks for drinking water and putting food into their mouths. Elephants travel in herds and the oldest female is usually the leader of the herd.

Giraffes are the tallest land mammals. They are so tall they can eat leaves from the tops of many trees. Giraffes have very long tongues, which they use to pull leaves off trees.

Bears are not as big as elephants, but they can still weigh up to 1,700 pounds (770 kg). Bears usually live by themselves. They eat plants and berries, but sometimes they eat small animals and fish.

Small mammals are also very interesting. The pika is a small animal that lives on rocky mountain slopes. Other small mammals include mice, voles, hamsters, and gerbils. You may have even owned one of these kinds of mammals as a pet.

Some mammals are very unusual. Bats are mammals that fly. You may think that a bat is a bird, but it has hair and does not have feathers so it cannot be a bird. Two other unusual mammals are the spiny anteater and the platypus. These two mammals lay eggs instead of giving birth to live babies. They are the only mammals that lay eggs. They nurse their babies and have hair on their bodies, so they are still considered mammals.

God has created many different mammals. Some are cute and cuddly, others look ferocious, but they are all special. Look at an animal encyclopedia or other animal book to see even more amazing mammals.

- **Name three large mammals.**
- **Name three small mammals.**
- **Name one mammal that can fly.**
- **Name one mammal that can lay eggs.**

The variety of mammals is astounding. God created hundreds of different kinds of mammals. Mammals live in nearly every part of the world including the oceans. We cannot possibly cover every kind of mammal in this book, but we will look at a few of the more interesting ones.

Among the largest land mammals are the elephant, the giraffe, and the brown bear. Elephants are the largest of the land mammals. Adult elephants can weigh as much as 6 tons and stand up to 10 feet (3 m) high at the shoulder. They have only a little hair around their ears and eyes, but they are still mammals. Female elephants, called cows, and baby elephants, called calves, travel in herds. The oldest female is usually the leader of the herd. Male elephants, called bulls, usually travel alone or with other bulls and only join the herd during mating season. Elephants have long trunks, which they use for drinking and for putting food into their mouths. They also have long teeth called tusks that can be used to dig for roots and to remove bark from trees. Elephants are very strong and are sometimes trained by people to carry heavy burdens.

Giraffes are the tallest land mammals. They can grow to be nearly 19 feet (5.8 m) tall. This allows giraffes to eat leaves from trees that other animals cannot reach. Being so tall also allows giraffes to see long distances so they can watch for danger. Giraffes can also run very quickly, up to 35 miles per hour (15.6 m/s), for a short period of time. Giraffes live in the African savanna or grassland. One of the most fascinating features of a giraffe is its long tongue, which can be up to 21 inches (53 cm) long!

Bears are another interesting group of land mammals. Grizzly bears are a type of brown bear. They live in parts of the northern United States and Canada. A grizzly can be up to 8 feet (2.4 m) long from head to rear and weigh about 800 pounds (360 kg). The Alaskan brown bear can be up to 10 feet (3 m) long and weigh as much as 1,700 pounds (770 kg). Bears usually live by themselves after they are about two years old. Bears will eat nearly anything. Although

most of a bear's diet consists of plants and berries, it will also eat small animals and fish. When the salmon are swimming upstream, many bears will gather at the edges of the rivers to catch and eat the fish. Bears are very active during the spring, summer, and fall, but they sleep most of the winter. During the fall, bears eat nearly constantly to store up enough fat to keep them alive during the winter. They also prepare a den where they will be sheltered from the harsh winter weather. Then they will sleep during the cold weather. When spring arrives, a very hungry bear emerges from its den and begins eating again.

Pika

In contrast to the large mammals are some very interesting small mammals. The pika is a small animal that lives on rocky mountain slopes. It grows to be about 8 inches (20 cm) long and is similar to rabbits and hares. Other small mammals include mice, voles, hamsters, and gerbils.

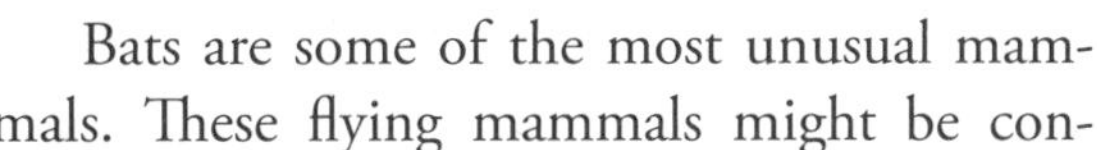

Bats are some of the most unusual mammals. These flying mammals might be confused with birds, but a closer examination will show that bats are very different from birds. Bats have hair, not feathers. And what appear to be wings are actually long fingers connected by a membrane that allows bats to fly. Bats are unusual also because they can detect objects by sending out high-pitched sound waves and sensing their reflections, somewhat like sonar.

Most mammals give birth to live babies, but two, the echidna (spiny anteater) and the platypus, are the only mammals that lay eggs. These animals are still considered mammals because they have mammary glands and nurse their young. They are warm-blooded, breathe air through lungs, and have hair as well.

God has created a wide variety of mammals. Many are cute and cuddly. Others are large and scary. But they are all part of the amazing world of animal. ■

Investigating Mammals

Choose a mammal that you want to learn more about. Then draw a picture of that mammal to include in your animal notebook.

For older children, research the animal you have chosen and write a report that answers as many of the following questions as possible.

1. What is this animal's habitat—where does it live?
2. How large does this animal grow to be?
3. What does this animal eat?
4. What enemies does this animal have?
5. How quickly does this animal reproduce? How many offspring does it have? How long is the mother pregnant? How long does the baby stay with the mother?
6. What other interesting things did you find out about your animal?

Add your picture and report to your animal notebook.

FUN FACT

You may not know this about mammals:

- Baby elephants sometimes suck their trunks in the same way that humans suck their thumbs.
- Elephants are pregnant longer than any other animal—22 months.
- Bears can get cavities from eating too much honey.
- A camel can drink 30 gallons of water in 13 minutes.
- The aye-aye is an animal that only lives on the island of Madagascar.
- The capybara is the world's largest rodent and can weigh 110 pounds (50 kg).

WHAT DID WE LEARN?

- What is the largest land mammal?
- What is the tallest land mammal?
- What do bears eat?

TAKING IT FURTHER

- What do you think is the most fascinating mammal? Why?

RUMINANTS

Another very interesting and important large mammal is the cow. Cattle are very important because of the milk and beef we get from them. Cattle are ruminants. **Ruminants** are animals that quickly eat their food without chewing it well. They later regurgitate their food and chew it very thoroughly before swallowing it again.

Ruminants have a four-chambered stomach. The first chamber is called the **rumen**. Here bacteria begin the process of digestion by beginning to break down the cellulose in the food. Some nutrients from the food are absorbed by the walls of the rumen. The food is then passed into the second chamber called the **reticulum**. The reticulum returns the food to the mouth for more chewing. At this point the food is called **cud** and the cow is said to "chew the cud" as it slowly chews up the food.

The cow then swallows the food for the second time. This time the food enters the third chamber of the stomach called the **omasum** where digestion continues. Much of the volatile fatty acids in the food is absorbed in the omasum. Water is also absorbed here.

The food finally enters the fourth chamber of the stomach called the **abomasum**, which is considered the true stomach. Here more digestive juices such as hydrochloric acid and enzymes are added and the food is further broken down.

Once the food leaves the stomach it enters the small intestine. Remaining nutrients are absorbed by the small intestine. What is not absorbed is passed into the large intestine where water is removed. Finally, the waste is expelled from the cow's body.

Ruminants have a very extensive digestive system because they have been designed to digest food that many other animals cannot eat. Grass, hay, and other feed are very difficult to digest, but the processes of chewing twice and fermenting in the rumen allow cattle and other ruminants to eat these foods. Other ruminants include goats, sheep, camels, oxen, and deer. Their digestive systems are another example of God's great design.

Draw a diagram of the ruminant digestive system. Be sure to label all the parts. Include this drawing in your notebook.

Monkeys & Apes

Primates

LESSON 5

What animals are classified as primates?

Words to know:

primates

binocular vision

New World monkeys

prehensile tail

Old World monkeys

apes

Beginners

Monkeys are always a favorite at the zoo. They are fun to watch with their silly antics as they play and swing from place to place. Monkeys are part of a group of mammals called **primates**. Monkeys and other primates have ten fingers and ten toes, and their eyes are on the front of their faces instead of on the sides of their faces like many other animals.

All monkeys have tails. Some monkeys can use their tails for climbing and holding on to branches, while other monkeys cannot. Monkeys are excellent climbers and spend much of their time in trees. They eat mostly fruits, flowers, and insects.

Other primates that are very similar to monkeys are the **apes**. You may have thought that apes were the same as monkeys, but there is one big difference. Apes do not have tails. Gorillas are the largest apes. Gorillas live in groups of ten or fewer. Chimpanzees are also apes. Chimps are very social and live in groups of up to 100 or more.

You might not be familiar with the third group of primates. These animals are called prosimians. Most prosimians live on an island called Madagascar. Lemurs and bushbabies are two kinds of prosimians. Most prosimians sleep during the day and are awake at night.

- **What group of mammals are monkeys a part of?**
- **What is the difference between monkeys and apes?**

- **Where do monkeys spend most of their time?**
- **What kinds of food do monkeys eat?**

Mandrill

Gorilla

Chimpanzee

One group of mammals that everyone enjoys watching at the zoo is the **primates**. Most people call these animals monkeys, but there are actually three different types of primates. Monkeys are the largest group of primates, but apes and prosimians are also primates. All primates share several common characteristics. First, they have ten fingers and ten toes. Also, primates have eyes on the front of their faces so they have **binocular vision**. Many other animals have eyes located more on the sides of their heads and therefore do not have the good depth perception that primates have.

There are around 160 different species of monkeys. Some are very small like the pygmy marmoset, which weighs only 8 ounces. The largest monkey is the mandrill, which can weigh as much as 100 pounds (45 kg). Monkeys live in Central and South America, Africa, and southern Asia. The monkeys that live in the western hemisphere are called **New World monkeys**. These monkeys are small to medium sized and have prehensile tails. A **prehensile tail** is one that is able to grasp onto things and can be used for climbing or swinging. **Old World monkeys** live in Africa and Asia. These monkeys are usually larger than the New World Monkeys and do not have prehensile tails.

Monkeys are excellent climbers, using their feet like a second set of hands. Monkeys spend most of their lives in trees and feed on leaves, fruit, flowers, and insects. A few monkeys prey on smaller animals.

The second group of primates is the apes. **Apes** are very similar to monkeys in appearance with one notable exception: apes do not have tails. Also, apes have arms that are longer than their legs. Common apes include gorillas, chimpanzees, orangutans, and gibbons. Apes live in the tropical forests of Africa and Southeast Asia. Unlike most monkeys, many apes spend a significant amount of time on the ground, although orangutans spend much of their time in the trees.

Gorillas are the largest apes. An adult male gorilla weighs about 350 pounds (160 kg) and an adult female weighs about

200 pounds (90 kg). Gorillas live in groups of 10 or fewer animals with one dominant male, several females, and several young gorillas that are not yet ready to live by themselves. When gorillas are mature they usually leave the group. A male will live by himself until he can find an unattached female to join him and begin a new group. A female will leave and join another group or a lone male.

Chimpanzees are very social apes. They live in groups of at least 12 and up to 100 members. They are mostly herbivorous and eat many different plants. However, they also eat termites and have even been known to eat other monkeys and small antelope. Chimps are very creative and use sticks and leaves to help collect termites and water. Other apes, such as orangutans, are less social and live more solitary lives.

The third group of primates is the prosimians. At first glance, prosimians may not seem to belong in the same category as apes and monkeys; however, they share the common characteristics of ten fingers and toes and binocular vision. Prosimians live mostly on the island of Madagascar, but some species live on mainland Africa and in southern Asia. There are 61 species of prosimians, including lemurs, tarsiers, lorises, and bushbabies. Most prosimians have very large eyes. This is helpful for hunting and seeing at night, which is when most prosimians are active. ■

Bushbaby

Lemur

Mammals Word Search

Complete the "Mammals Word Search." Put the word search in your animal notebook.

WHAT DID WE LEARN?

- What are two common characteristics of all primates?
- What are the three groups of primates?
- What is one difference between apes and monkeys?
- Where do New World Monkeys live?
- Where do Old World Monkeys live?
- What is a prehensile tail?

TAKING IT FURTHER

- If a monkey lives in South America is it likely to have a prehensile tail?
- Are you more likely to find a monkey or an ape in a tree in the rain forest?
- Why do most prosimians have very large eyes?

Ape Intelligence

Many people claim that man and primates such as monkeys and apes are close relatives because they have so much in common. They also point out that primates, and especially apes, are very intelligent so they must be related to humans.

Several tests have been done to see just how intelligent apes are. In one test, a chimpanzee was given a stick to play with. Later a banana was placed just out of reach of the chimp. At first the chimp expressed frustration and shook the bars of its cage. But eventually, the chimp used the stick to bring the fruit closer, thus showing the ability to reason and solve problems. Other animals have been shown to have similar reasoning abilities.

Apes have also been taught sign language. Several studies have been conducted with various apes including chimpanzees, orangutans, and gorillas. These apes have been taught to make signs to represent various objects, feelings, and ideas. Although they use these signs for communication, there is great disagreement about whether this is real language. Several of the studies have been shown to be flawed, revealing that the apes were really just making signs to receive some sort of compensation. Other studies claim that the apes truly communicate original ideas with their signs. However, the apes fail to develop true language with grammar structure. This ability is limited to humans only. René Descartes, the famous philosopher/mathematician, believed that language was what separated humans who have souls from animals who do not.

It is true that animals have intelligence. God designed them that way. This is one thing that makes animals so interesting. However, there is a fundamental difference between animals and humans as pointed out by Descartes. Humans have souls and can commune with God. So even if your ape can say hello in sign language, that does not make him your brother.

God designed animals to be intelligent, to even reason and solve problems to a limited extent.

Special FEATURE

Man & Monkeys

Did man descend from the apes?

Nearly every library book you pick up about monkeys says that they are relatives of man or that man and monkeys descended from a common ancestor. They point out that humans and apes have many common characteristics so it makes sense that they have common roots. However, the Bible tells a very different story. The Bible says that God formed man from the dust of the ground and woman from man's rib (Genesis 2:7, 22). It also states that people are made in God's own image (Genesis 1:26–27). Humans are a result of God's miracle of creation, not an accident of nature or a series of genetic mutations.

For many years evolutionists have been trying to find the "missing link" between apes and humans. If a fossil of a creature that was partway between a man and an ape could be found, they say, it would be very powerful evidence for the theory of evolution. And several claims have been made that the "missing link" has been found. However, when each of these claims has been carefully examined, none has been shown to be something that is half ape and half man. Many examples have been shown to be either just an ape or just a human. Sadly, some examples have been shown to be frauds. Let's look at the most famous examples of "missing links."

One of the earliest supposed examples of an ape-man was the Neanderthal Man. In 1856 a few fragments of fossils were discovered in Neander Valley, Germany. Then, in 1908, a nearly complete skeleton of a Neanderthal was discovered in France. This skeleton was of a creature with a skull very much like a human (but with a larger brain case), but who did not walk completely upright. From this discovery, many scientists claimed that Neanderthal Man was subhuman. However, later it was discovered that this skeleton and other bones found in the same area showed that the people suffered from arthritis and from rickets, a disease that causes bones to become deformed. Other Neanderthal skeletons have been discovered that indicate they walked upright and have completely human characteristics, and it has been shown that they made musical instruments, buried their dead, and had language capabilities.

Neanderthal Man has been shown to be just a man. Most biblical creationists believe Neanderthal Man was a unique variant of modern man who lived in Europe and adjacent Asia and North Africa after the Babel dispersion during the Ice Age.

In 1912 some fossils were discovered near Piltdown, England. These bones included pieces of a jawbone and a skull. Scientists examining the bones declared that the bones were all from one creature that had both human and ape characteristics. This sample was called the Piltdown Man. However, in 1950 scientists declared Piltdown Man to be a hoax. Someone had taken a human skull bone and an ape jawbone and stained them to make them look old. They had also filed the teeth in the jawbone to make them look more human. These "fossils" were then planted in a gravel pit where they were sure to be discovered. Piltdown Man was a fraud.

Nebraska Man was discovered in 1922 in western Nebraska. This discovery consisted of a single tooth, yet scientists declared that it proved the existence of an ape-like man or a man-like ape. The *Illustrated London News* even published a picture of Nebraska Man along with his wife and the tools they used. However, later expeditions unearthed other bones of the supposed ape-man and scientists discovered that the tooth actually belonged to a pig. Nebraska Man was just wishful thinking and bad science.

One of the most famous supposed "missing links" is Lucy. Lucy was discovered by Dr. Donald Johanson in Ethiopia in 1973. This skeleton supposedly shows an ape-like creature that walked upright and thus was an ancestor, or relative, of humans. However, there is great controversy surrounding Lucy. First, Lucy has a lower jaw bone (mandible) that closely resembles that of a gorilla—not that of a human or even a chimp. Second, Lucy's wrist structure has been shown to be consistent with other apes that walk using their knuckles for balance. And third, other skulls that are of the same species as Lucy have been tested and show inner ear characteristics of creatures that do not walk upright.

People are often misled by inaccurately reconstructed statues and images of Lucy displayed at museums and in textbooks, as her feet and hands are often portrayed as being very human-like. Lucy, however, had long curved fingers and toes, similar to modern apes, and a big toe that sticks out to the side, as in chimpanzees. Most scientists now believe that Lucy is simply the skeleton of an extinct species of ape.

No discoveries have been made that show a direct link between apes and humans. The missing links are still missing and will remain missing because God created man and apes separately. So, the next time you pick up a book that says that man is a descendant of an ape, you can ask where the evidence is for that idea. Because the real evidence clearly indicates that apes are apes and humans are humans. You can believe the Bible.

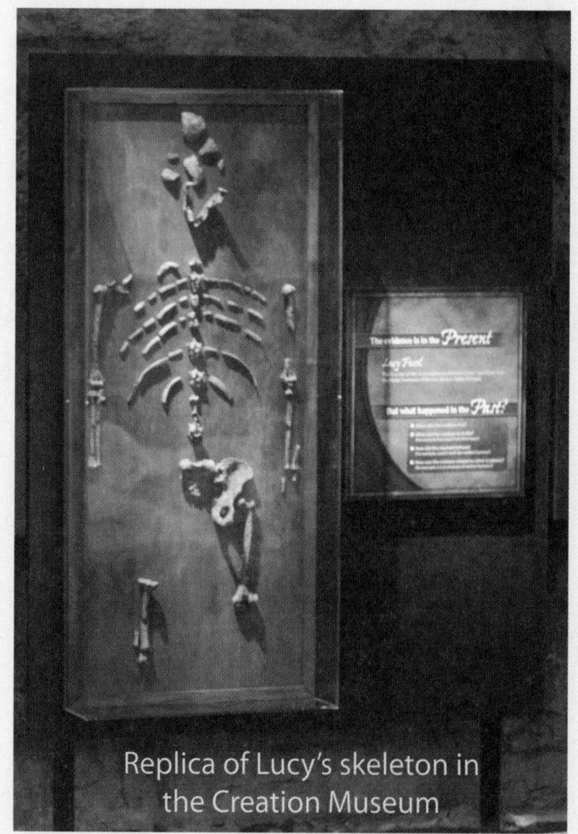

Replica of Lucy's skeleton in the Creation Museum

Aquatic Mammals

They live in the water?

Lesson 6

How are whales and dolphins different from fish?

Words to know:

fluke

blowhole

baleen

keratin

rostrum

Challenge words:

rorqual

echolocation

Beginners

Have you ever seen a dolphin jump out of the water? Did you think it was a big fish? Dolphins and whales look very much like fish, but they are not fish. They are actually mammals that live in the water.

Dolphins and whales are different from fish in some very important ways. First, dolphins and whales breathe air using their lungs, but fish get air from water using gills. Second, dolphins and whales give birth to live babies and nurse their babies after they are born. Fish, however, lay eggs and do not nurse their young. Finally, dolphins and whales are warm-blooded, but fish are cold-blooded.

God specially designed dolphins and whales to live in the water. First, they have a special hole called a **blowhole** on the tops of their heads. This allows them to breathe quickly when they reach the surface of the water. These animals also have special tails that allow them to dive and move through the water very quickly.

Dolphins and whales are very special mammals that live in the water. So the next time you are at the ocean, look for mammals as well as fish.

- **What is different about how dolphins and whales breathe compared to how fish breathe?**
- **What is different about how dolphins and whales feed their babies compared to how fish feed their babies?**
- **What feature do dolphins and whales have to help them breathe?**

When people think of mammals they generally think of furry animals that live on land. They think of monkeys, mice, and tigers. However, not all mammals live on the land. There are several mammals that live in the ocean. These include dolphins, porpoises, and whales. These animals are often thought of as large fish. However, whales, porpoises, and dolphins all breathe with lungs and must come to the surface for air on a regular basis. Also, they give birth to live young and nurse their young. Fish cannot do any of these things. In addition, dolphins, porpoises, and whales are warm-blooded while fish are cold-blooded.

Whale fluke as seen above water

Dolphins, porpoises, and whales all have bodies that were designed for living in the water. God gave these mammals sleek bodies that easily glide through the water as well as powerful tail fins, called **flukes**. The fluke moves up and down, instead of side to side like a fish's tail, allowing the animal to dive deep into the water and then resurface quickly for breathing. Because they are designed by God to live in the water, whales, porpoises, and dolphins do not breathe through a nose like most land animals. Instead, each has an opening on the top of its head called a **blowhole** through which it breathes. When the animal surfaces, it exhales the air in its lungs causing a spurt of air and a small amount of water to shoot into the sky before the animal takes a new breath.

There are about 90 species of whales, porpoises, and dolphins. Dolphins, porpoises, and many species of whales have teeth. Other species of whales have large

Dolphins have rostrums and a wave-shaped dorsal fin.

Manatee

comb-like structures in their mouths that they use for straining food from the water. These structures are called **baleen** and are made from **keratin**, the same material that your hair and fingernails are made from. Some whales use their baleen to strain out fish and other animals. But the blue whale, which is the largest animal on earth, eats krill, tiny shrimp-like creatures, which are some of the smallest animals on earth. Of course, a blue whale eats about 8,000 pounds (3,600 kg) of krill each day!

What is the difference between dolphins and porpoises? In comparison to dolphins, porpoises are very small. Porpoises seldom exceed 7 feet (2 m) in length, whereas many dolphins can be more than 10 feet (3 m) in length. Dolphins have a lean sleek body, whereas porpoises often appear chubby. The dorsal fin (the fin on the animal's back) in porpoises is triangular, looking more like a shark, while the dorsal fin of the dolphin is shaped like a wave. Porpoises are blunt-nosed, lacking a **rostrum**, or beak, which is very prominent in dolphins.

Another mammal that spends its entire life in the water is a manatee. Manatees, which somewhat resemble seals or walruses, live in areas with warm water such as the Florida Everglades and many of the rivers of South America. The manatee, and its relative the dugong, is a gentle, slow moving creature that grazes on sea grasses. This grazing habit is often compared to cattle grazing and the manatee is often called a sea cow. Manatees spend most of the time eating and can eat a pound of grass for every ten pounds of their weight each day. That means that a 600-pound (270 kg) manatee would eat 60 pounds (27 kg) of plants a day! Like the whales and dolphins, the manatee also has a tail that moves

Fun Fact

Some people believe that the legend of mermaids swimming in the ocean may have come from sailors who saw manatees slowly swimming below the surface of the water.

Acting Like a Whale

Activity 1

Aquatic mammals live their entire lives in the water, yet they breathe air so they must surface periodically to get a fresh breath. A porpoise can hold its breath for about 4 minutes. Manatees can stay submerged for up to 6 minutes at a time. A bottlenose dolphin can stay underwater for up to 15 minutes. But when it comes to staying submerged, the king of underwater mammals is the sperm whale, which can hold its breath for an hour or more. How long can you hold your breath?

Purpose: To appreciate how long animals can hold their breath

Materials: stopwatch

Procedure:

1. Use a stop watch to time how long you can hold your breath.

Activity 2

Baleen whales do not have teeth. Instead, they have comb-like ridges, called baleen, that trap food from the water.

Purpose: To understand how baleen whales get their food

Materials: nuts, fruits, vegetables, knife, toothbrush, two cups, water

Procedure:

1. Chop some nuts, fruits, or vegetables into tiny pieces.
2. Add the pieces to a cup of water. The chopped food represents the tiny creatures that live in the ocean.
3. Hold a toothbrush sideways over an empty cup and slowly pour the water and food mixture through the bristles of the toothbrush. The bristles will catch some of the food pieces.
4. Pull the pieces out of the toothbrush and eat them just like the whale pulls food out of its baleen with its tongue.

up and down to help it swim and dive. And although the manatee does not have a blowhole, God gave it nostrils on the top of its head so it can surface for air while keeping the majority of its body submerged in water.

God designed most mammals to live on land, but a few were designed to live in the water. The next time you go to the ocean, keep your eyes open for mammals as well as fish. ■

What Did We Learn?

- Why are dolphins and whales considered mammals and not fish?
- What is the main difference between the tails of fish and the tails of aquatic mammals?
- What is another name for a manatee?
- Why are manatees sometimes called this?

Taking It Further

- How has God specially designed aquatic mammals for breathing air?
- What do you think might be one of the first things a mother whale or dolphin must teach a newborn baby?

Amazing Whales

Whales are some of the most amazing creatures in the world. When you learn about whales you see that God designed them with many special features. For example, land mammals have a connection between their mouths and their noses, but there is no connection between a whale's blowhole and its mouth. God designed the whale this way so that it can open its mouth to feed and not have a chance of water entering its lungs.

The blue whale is the largest creature ever created. Even the largest dinosaurs were small compared to the blue whale. A blue whale can be up to 100 feet (30 m) long and weigh up to 300,000 pounds (135,000 kg). The fin whale is the second largest creature reaching lengths up to 80 feet (24 m). These whales, which are part of the **rorqual** family of whales, have special grooved throats that expand as they eat, allowing these giant mammals to eat tons of tiny krill (small shrimp-like animals) each day.

Many whales use **echolocation**, or sonar, for communication. They send out sound waves. When these sound waves bump up against something they bounce off. The whale can detect the bounced waves and determine where the object is. Whales use their echolocation to communicate with other whales. They also use this process to find prey. This is similar to how bats locate prey.

Sperm whales are the deepest diving whales. They can dive up to 10,000 feet (3,050 m) below the surface and can dive up to 550 feet per minute (2.8 m/s). The water pressure increases one atmosphere for every 33 feet (10 m) that you go below the surface of the water, so as they dive, the water pressure on their bodies quickly increases. Sperm whales can experience a change of 15 atmospheres of pressure in less than a minute, and the pressure on the whale's head can be two or three times the pressure on its tail. You might expect this to be a problem for the whale. It is certainly a problem for humans who dive quickly and then resurface quickly. But God designed the sperm whale's body to compensate for these extreme pressure changes. The sperm whale can shut down parts of its circulatory system to send extra blood to areas that need higher pressure, and it can closely regulate the pressure in various blood vessels throughout its body.

The sperm whale can hold its breath for an hour or more. This allows it to dive deeply to find its main food, the giant squid. Once it reaches the bottom where the squid live, the sperm whale can shut down nearly every body function while it eats so that it can stay submerged long enough to eat its fill before needing to surface for more air.

Humpback whales also have interesting design features. The fins of a humpback whale have many blood vessels close to the surface. This allows the whales to use their fins to help control their body temperature. They move their fins back and forth in the water and sometimes in the air to cool their bodies.

Whales are truly designed by God to be well suited for their environment. See what other interesting things you can find out about whales that demonstrate God's special design.

Humpback whale

MARSUPIALS

Pouched animals

LESSON 7

How are marsupials different from other mammals?

Words to know:

marsupial

joey

nocturnal

BEGINNERS

Kangaroos are some of the funniest animals to watch. They hop instead of walking or running, and they box each other for a mate. Kangaroos are often seen with a baby sticking its head out of a pouch on the mother's belly. Kangaroos are part of a group of mammals called **marsupials**.

Marsupials are animals that have pouches. When a kangaroo or other marsupial baby is born it is very tiny and does not look like its parents at all. This tiny baby is called a **joey**. A joey looks more like a little worm than a kangaroo; it is hairless and blind. Shortly after it is born, it finds its way to its mother's pouch where it attaches itself to a nipple and nurses and grows for several months. Nearly all marsupials live in Australia, Tasmania, and New Zealand. The opossum is the only marsupial that lives in North America.

Kangaroos are the most famous marsupials. Kangaroos have large hind legs and very large feet that are perfect for hopping. Kangaroos can hop faster than many animals can run. Kangaroos are usually awake at night and sleep during the day.

Koalas, opossums, and kangaroos all eat plants, but some marsupials eat meat. Numbats eat ants and termites, and Tasmanian devils eat larger animals such as sheep and rabbits.

- **What feature is special about a marsupial?**

- **What is a newborn marsupial called?**
- **Name three marsupials.**
- **What time of the day are kangaroos usually awake?**

Of all the mammals in the world, one of the most entertaining is the kangaroo. Kangaroos hop faster than many animals can run. Kangaroos box each other in a fight for a mate. And kangaroos are often seen with the head of a baby poking out of a pouch. These entertaining animals that God created are part of a group of mammals called **marsupials**.

Kangaroo

Marsupials are mammals that give birth to babies that are not fully developed. These tiny babies, depending on the species, can be as small as a grain of rice or as big as a bumble bee. A newly-born baby is called a **joey** and is naked and blind. It uses its sense of smell to crawl along its mother's belly searching for the pouch that will protect it until it is fully developed. Once the joey reaches the pouch, it crawls inside and attaches itself to its mother's mammary gland where it will remain, nursing and growing, for several months.

Kangaroos are the most famous marsupials, but there are many other pouched mammals as well. Koalas, numbats, mulgaras, and Tasmanian devils are some of the over 260 species of marsupials. Nearly all marsupials live in Australia, Tasmania, and New Zealand. The only marsupial known to live in North America is the opossum.

The opossum is North America's only marsupial.

Red kangaroos are the largest of the kangaroos and can be up to 8 feet (2.4 m) tall. They are the largest hopping animals on earth. Yet some breeds of kangaroos are very small. The musky rat kangaroo is only 10–12 inches (25–30 cm) high. But big or small, all kangaroos have large hind legs with big hind feet. The middle toe of each hind foot is longer than the others and is used for pushing off when hopping. Also, all kangaroos have large tails that help them keep their balance.

FUN FACT

A red kangaroo can hop up to 30 feet (9 m) in one leap.

Large kangaroos can hop at speeds up to 30–35 mph (13–16 m/s). God designed the kangaroo to be a hopping machine. The large legs and tail are ideal. And at the back of each leg is a long stretchy tendon attaching the muscles of the leg to the ankle bones. This tendon stores up energy between hops that is released when the feet hit the ground. When a kangaroo is hopping, its body remains at about the same height, while its legs stretch out and then fold up as

Making a Pouch

Purpose: To make your own marsupial pouch

Materials: tag board, zipper bag, scissors, pencil, glue, fake fur or felt

Procedure:

1. On a sheet of tag board or construction paper, draw the belly of a kangaroo.
2. In the center of the sheet, glue a plastic zipper bag with the zipper side up.
3. Now glue fake fur or felt across the outside of the zipper bag. Be sure that the fur completely covers the sides and bottom of the zipper bag, but does not block the top of the bag. You now have a pouch.
4. If you have enough fur, you can glue it on the rest of the paper to make the pouch blend in with the belly of the kangaroo.
5. Next, use tag board or construction paper to make a baby kangaroo. You can zip and unzip the pouch just like a mother kangaroo tightens and loosens the muscles of her pouch to protect her baby. You many even want to make various sizes of babies. When a joey first enters the pouch it is smaller than a bumblebee, has no hair, and its eyes are sealed shut. It grows and develops in the pouch. When it is big enough, it leaves and reenters the pouch until it is too big to crawl back inside. Add your pouch and joey to your animal notebook.

it hops. God designed the kangaroo so well for hopping that it uses up about the same amount of energy when it is hopping slowly as when it is hopping quickly.

Kangaroos are generally **nocturnal**, meaning they are active at night. They spend most of the day sleeping and resting. Then, when the sun goes down and the temperatures cool off, kangaroos begin eating, which they continue doing almost the entire time they are awake. Kangaroos are plant eaters, and like many other plant eaters, they chew their food and swallow it, then later, they spit the food back up and chew it some more. Kangaroos also have special bacteria living in their digestive tracts that eat the cellulose in the plants and help the kangaroos digest the plants.

Koalas, opossums, and kangaroos are all plant eaters. But many other marsupials are insect or meat eaters. The numbat is a marsupial that eats ants and termites. The numbat uses its sharp claws to tear open trees or termite hills. Then it uses its sticky 4-inch (10 cm) long tongue to pick up termites or ants for a tasty meal. A hungry numbat can eat as many as 20,000 termites in one day.

The most famous meat-eating marsupial is the Tasmanian devil. Thanks to its sharp teeth and tendency to growl, it has earned a reputation as a very fierce animal.

Fun Fact

A female kangaroo is ready to mate at about two years old. From that time on she will be nearly always pregnant. In fact, she will often have a baby in her womb, a baby in her pouch, and a youngster at her side all at the same time.

However, recent studies have shown that it is not as fierce as once believed. Tasmanian devils live only on the island of Tasmania near Australia. These animals are nocturnal and live in brushy, wooded areas. They hunt wallabies, wombats, sheep, and rabbits. But they prefer to eat animals that are already dead instead of hunting. Like all marsupials, Tasmanian devils give birth to very tiny young, usually weighing only a fraction of an ounce. The joey then moves to the mother's pouch where it lives and grows for the next 15 weeks.

Tasmanian devil

FUN FACT

Kangaroos keep cool by panting like a dog. When it is really hot, a kangaroo will lick its forearms and the evaporation of the saliva will help to cool down the kangaroo.

From numbats to opossums, marsupials are very interesting creatures. See what else you can learn about these pouched animals. ■

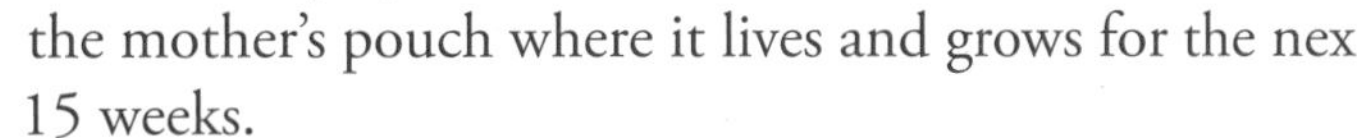

WHAT DID WE LEARN?

- What is a marsupial?
- Name at least three marsupials.
- How has God designed the kangaroo for jumping?

TAKING IT FURTHER

- About half of a kangaroo's body weight is from muscle. This is nearly twice as much as in most animals its size. How might this fact contribute to its ability to hop?
- How do you think a joey kangaroo keeps from falling out of its mother's pouch when she hops?

KOALAS

Koalas are one of Australia's most famous animals and they are marsupials. See how much you can find out about koalas from an animal encyclopedia or from an online source. Then fill out the "Koala Fun Facts" worksheet.

UNIT 2

BIRDS & FISH

- ◊ **Explain** how birds were designed for flight.
- ◊ **Describe** the unique characteristics of birds and fish using examples.
- ◊ **Distinguish** between warm-blooded and cold-blooded animals.

KEY CONCEPTS | UNIT LESSONS

Birds

Fine feathered friends

LESSON 8

What features make birds different from all other animals?

Words to know:

talon

Beginners

Birds are some of the easiest animals to watch. They live nearly everywhere and often fly into our backyards. Birds are different from all other animals because they have feathers. Birds keep the same body temperature all the time so they are warm-blooded animals. Birds lay eggs and breathe air with lungs. All of these features make birds special.

God designed birds so that they are great flyers. God also gave birds special beaks and feet so they can survive well where they live. Birds that perch in trees have special toes for grasping the tree limbs and pointed beaks for eating seeds. Sparrows and bluebirds are perching birds.

Other birds, like eagles, have sharp beaks and claws that help them capture the mice and other animals they eat. Birds that live in the water, like ducks, have wide beaks or bills, and webbed feet that help them swim and catch their food in the water.

Some birds, such as the ostrich, do not fly, but can run across the ground. These birds have specially designed feet that allow them to move quickly on land. Look at the pictures in this book and other animal books to see the different beaks and feet that birds have.

- **What feature makes birds different from all other animals?**
- **How do birds breathe?**
- **How do birds give birth?**
- **How did God make birds' beaks and feet to help them survive?**

Birds are some of the most interesting and easy to watch animals in God's creation. These warm-blooded, feathered vertebrates can be found in every region of the world. There are approximately 9,000 different species of birds (but far fewer created "kinds" of birds). Birds lay eggs and breathe with lungs. Most birds are excellent flyers, although some birds do not fly. God designed birds' bodies to be efficient flying machines. Birds have strong yet lightweight bones; many bones have hollow spaces to make them lighter. Birds also have rigid or stiff backbones that support the strong muscles used to move the wings.

Fun Fact

There are between 100 and 200 billion birds on the planet.

Perching bird

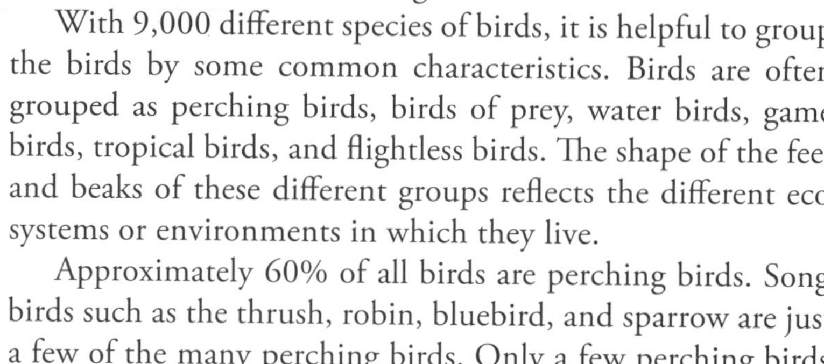

With 9,000 different species of birds, it is helpful to group the birds by some common characteristics. Birds are often grouped as perching birds, birds of prey, water birds, game birds, tropical birds, and flightless birds. The shape of the feet and beaks of these different groups reflects the different ecosystems or environments in which they live.

Bird of prey

Approximately 60% of all birds are perching birds. Songbirds such as the thrush, robin, bluebird, and sparrow are just a few of the many perching birds. Only a few perching birds, such as the hummingbird and woodpecker, do not have songs. Perching birds have feet with 3 toes facing forward and 1 toe facing backward for grasping branches. Many have triangular-shaped pointed beaks for eating seeds and insects. Some of these birds, such as hummingbirds, have long narrow beaks for sucking nectar from flowers.

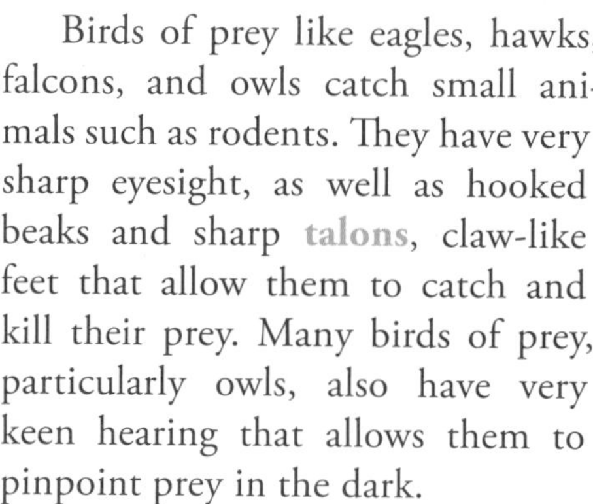

Birds of prey like eagles, hawks, falcons, and owls catch small animals such as rodents. They have very sharp eyesight, as well as hooked beaks and sharp **talons**, claw-like feet that allow them to catch and kill their prey. Many birds of prey, particularly owls, also have very keen hearing that allows them to pinpoint prey in the dark.

Water bird

Water birds, such as ducks, swans, and geese, are specially designed for life on and near the water. They have

Fun Fact

The smallest bird is the bee hummingbird from Cuba, which weighs only 0.056 ounces (1.6 g)—less than a penny.

Bird Beaks & Bird Feet

Examine the pictures in this lesson as well as pictures of birds in other books to get a better idea of how different birds' beaks and feet look. Then fill out the "Bird Beaks and Feet" worksheet by drawing the different types of beaks and feet that birds have.

Notice the various uses of the different shaped beaks and feet and how they help the birds to survive in their environment. Add this page to your animal notebook.

Other Optional Activities

1. Put up a bird feeder and enjoy watching the birds come close on a regular basis.
2. Find abandoned nests and dissect them to find out what birds use to build their nests.

Fun Fact

The heaviest flying bird is the Andean condor at 30 pounds (13.5 kg).

rounded beaks for catching fish and other food in the water, and they have webbed feet for swimming. They also secrete oil that helps make their feathers water resistant.

Game birds are birds that are often hunted for meat. They have very strong flight muscles making them difficult to catch but good to eat once they are caught. These include wild turkey, quail, and pheasant. Although ducks and geese are considered water birds, they are game birds as well.

Game bird

Tropical bird

Tropical birds include parrots, parakeets, and toucans. These birds live in the tropical rain forests. Most are very brightly colored and have large hooked beaks. They have similar feet to perching birds since they spend most of their time in the trees.

Finally, a few birds are flightless. These birds have wings but are not able to fly. Flightless birds include ostriches, emus, and penguins. These birds are designed for their lifestyle, being able to run or swim very swiftly. ■

What did we learn?

- How do birds differ from mammals?
- How are birds the same as mammals?

Taking it further

- How can you identify one bird from another?
- What birds can you identify near your home?
- Why might you see different birds near your home in the summer than in the winter?

Birds vs. Reptiles

Studying birds' beaks can be very interesting. In fact, one scientist, Charles Darwin, became famous when he made some detailed observations about the beaks of finches in the Galapagos Islands. Darwin observed that finches in one area had beaks that were larger and a different shape than ones in a different area. The size and shape of beaks of the various types of finches seemed related to the food available where the birds lived. Darwin concluded that this was a result of natural selection; the birds with the beaks that were well suited for their environment survived better than the others so they became the dominant species in that area.

This part of Darwin's theory is well supported by what we observe today. We see an animal with a particular trait surviving better than the same kind of animal without that trait. However, Darwin, and many scientists that have followed him, extended this observation to conclude that one kind of animal can change into another kind of animal by natural selection. We do not observe this happening today and there is no conclusive evidence in the fossil record that it has happened in the past.

Many evolutionists claim that the birds we see today have evolved from reptiles, possibly dinosaurs, in the past. Let's look at what kinds of changes would be needed for that to happen. First, birds are warm-blooded and reptiles are cold-blooded. A system would need to be developed to allow the animal in between a bird and a reptile to regulate its body temperature. But it is unknown how this could happen in small progressive steps that are required by Darwin's theory. A system that was not fully functional would be useless and would not provide any known benefit.

Second, the animal would have to develop a much larger brain. On average, birds' brains are much larger than reptiles' brains. Also, the circulatory and respiratory systems are very different between birds and reptiles. We will look at this in more detail in lesson 10.

Finally, feathers and scales are very different. There is no known way to change a scale into a feather through small changes. So we see that it is very difficult to believe that a reptile changed into a bird, even given the supposed millions of years.

Instead of thinking about evolution when we see variety among birds' beaks, we need to think of God's wonderful creativity that made such variety. We see this variety among many kinds of birds. There are many different sparrows, each with distinct coloring, songs, and habits, yet they are all sparrows that came from the sparrows that were on Noah's ark. They look different because God created the original animals with the information to produce many different looking offspring, but their offspring are all still sparrows.

List some characteristics that may vary among an animal kind due to natural selection. Look through an animal encyclopedia to see examples of these characteristics. Notice that none of these various characteristics has resulted in a new kind of animal.

Fun Fact

The largest bird is the ostrich, which can be up to 9 feet (2.7 m) tall and weigh as much as 300 pounds (136 kg).

Charles Darwin

1809–1882

The name Charles Darwin can evoke strong emotions. Some people view him as one of the greatest scientists of the 19th century. Others see him as the man who destroyed our belief in God. Regardless of how you feel about evolution and creation, it is important to know what Darwin did and to examine his findings in light of the Bible and in light of modern science. Charles Darwin was born in Shrewsbury, England in 1809. His father was a doctor and his mother was the daughter of the famous china maker, Josiah Wedgwood.

After earning a degree in theology in 1831, Darwin was selected to be part of a nature tour around the world. From 1831–1839 he sailed from place to place on the ship HMS *Beagle*. At each place he visited, Darwin carefully studied and collected plants, animals, rocks, and fossils. He is most famous for his study of the finches of the Galapagos Islands. He discovered that different species of finches on each island had different beaks depending on the type of diet available there. This led him to seek an explanation for how such variety could occur.

In 1859, after years of study, Darwin published his most famous work, *On the Origin of Species*. In this work, Darwin suggested that changes within species were a result of natural selection—survival of the fittest. This idea was taken further to suggest that over time these small changes could result in a completely new kind of animal. Later, in 1871, Darwin published a book called *The Descent of Man*, in which he suggested that man evolved from ape-like ancestors.

It is important to note that Darwin knew nothing about genetics or how traits were passed from one generation to the next. We know today that animals have a wide variety of traits that are passed on through their genes. We can see this variety in the many species of dogs that exist today (wolf, fox, coyote, domestic dog, etc.). However, we also know that there is a limit to the amount of change that can occur genetically. Evolutionists claim that mutations in the genes can result in new information for new structures and organs, and that if these mutations help the organism survive, they are passed on to their offspring. However, no one has ever observed a mutation that added new information to the genes. All observed mutations have been determined to be harmful or neutral to the animal, and result in a loss of information.

We can observe adaptation, such as Darwin observed with his finches, but we do not see changes that change one kind of animal into another. Furthermore, no fossil evidence has been found to show a progression of changes from one kind of animal into another. What we observe in both nature and in the fossil record is that a finch is still a finch and a dog is still a dog. God created each type of animal with a wonderful capacity for variety within its kind, but there is no evidence of evolution from one kind to another.

Flight

How do those birds do that?

Lesson 9

How are feathers used by birds?

Words to know:

airfoil

down feathers

contour feathers

flight feathers

preening

Challenge words:

casque

Beginners

Do you enjoy watching birds fly through the air? Most birds can fly. God designed birds' bodies especially for flight. Birds have very strong breast muscles and stiff backbones so they can strongly flap their wings. They also have air spaces inside their bones so that they are lighter, which makes it easier for them to fly.

A bird's wing is the most important feature that helps a bird fly. Its wing has a special shape that allows the air to flow around it and lift the bird up. The wing is also covered with special feathers that help the bird to fly. These feathers all point toward the back of the bird so that air flows smoothly over the feathers as the bird is flying.

Finally, the bird can move its tail back and forth to help it steer as it is flying through the air. The tail acts just like a rudder on a ship. God made birds just right for flying.

- **Name three things that help a bird to fly.**
- **Why is it important that a bird's feathers point toward the back of the bird?**
- **How does a bird use its tail while it is flying?**

Although some birds are flightless, most birds are designed for flight. To watch a bird soaring into the sky is a marvelous thing. For centuries man sought to imitate birds, but only in the last 100 years or so has man truly begun to understand how perfectly designed the bird's body is for flight.

Birds have very strong breast muscles attached to wide sternums, and they have stiff backbones to withstand the forces of flight. The muscles help move the wings smoothly and efficiently. Birds also have a special respiratory system that allows them to breathe air through lungs into a system of air sacs that extract much more oxygen than any other animal's respiratory system can. Birds have hollow spaces in their bones, making them extremely light for their size. These and many other special features aid birds in flying.

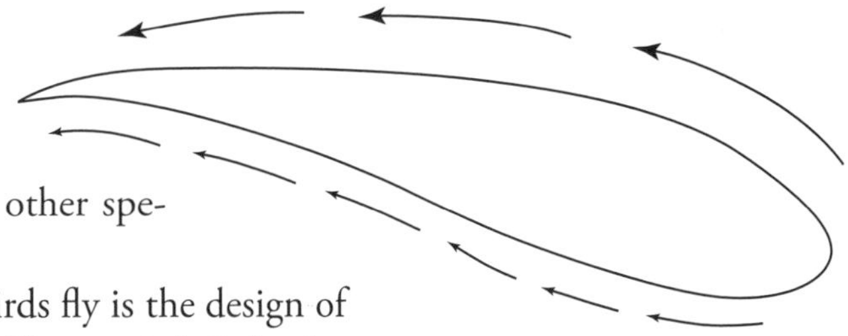

By far the most important feature to help birds fly is the design of their wings and feathers. Their wings are shaped like an **airfoil**, forcing air to flow more quickly over the wings than under them. This creates lower pressure over the wings, thus creating lift.

Birds have three kinds of feathers, each with a different function. Soft fuzzy **down feathers** provide insulation near the bird's body. Over these are the **contour feathers** that cover the bird's body. All contour feathers point toward the tail, making air flow smoothly over the bird's body. **Flight feathers** give the wing the needed shape for flying. Feathers are designed with a hook and barb system to help the feather maintain its shape. If a feather gets pulled apart the bird can zip it back up with its beak. This is called **preening**.

A bird's wing has three sets of flight feathers. The primary feathers are attached near the end of the wing; the secondary feathers are attached in the center;

Fun Fact

Hummingbirds have the fastest wing-beat of all birds. Their wings can complete more than 75 up and down movements in a second.

Examining a Bird's Feather

Examine a bird's feather with a magnifying glass. Notice the barbs that hold the feather together. A bird can "zip up" its feathers with its beak if they get pulled open. This is called preening. Birds spend some time every day fixing or preening their feathers.

Wing & Feather Worksheet

Fill out the "God Designed Birds To Fly" worksheet by drawing an airfoil, labeling the feathers on the bird's wing, and drawing an example of the structure of a feather. Glue the bird's feather to the sheet. Add this page to your animal notebook.

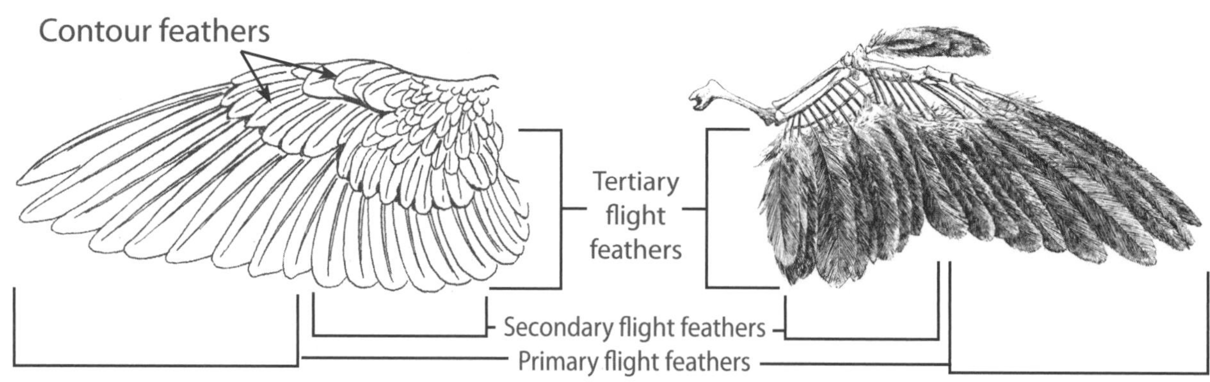

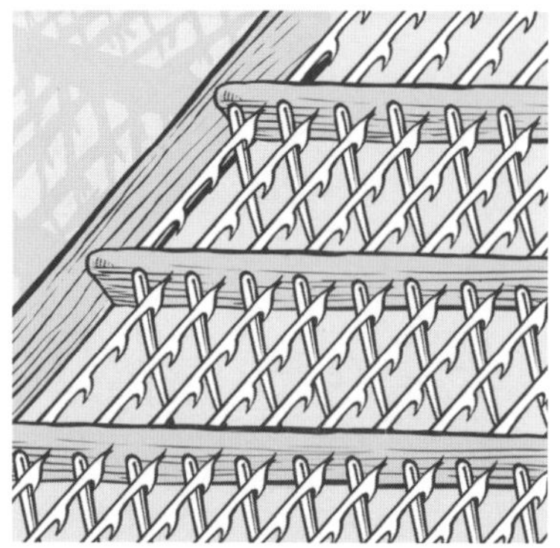
A hook-and-barb system holds the feather together.

and the tertiary feathers are attached to the upper wing, close to the body. Movement of the flight feathers makes tiny changes in the shape of the wing to compensate for changing air conditions. Contour feathers on the front of the wing make a smooth surface over which the air can easily flow.

Finally, the bird's tail serves as a rudder. By moving the tail from side to side, the bird can steer or change direction in the air. God designed every part of the bird for efficient flight. ■

Fun Fact

The peregrine falcon is perhaps the fastest animal on earth. In a stoop, or dive, the peregrine has been clocked at speeds of over 180 mph (80.5 m/s).

WHAT DID WE LEARN?

- What are some ways birds are designed for flight?
- What are the three kinds of bird feathers?
- How does a bird repair a feather that is pulled open?
- How does a bird's tail work like a rudder?

TAKING IT FURTHER

- Why can't man fly by strapping wings to his arms?
- How do you think birds use their feathers to stay warm?
- How is an airplane wing like a bird's wing?

Flightless birds

Although most birds were designed to fly, about one percent of all birds are flightless. Probably the most well know flightless bird is the ostrich. The ostrich is the largest bird in the world. Although it cannot fly, it can run up to 45 mph (72 km/h). The ostrich has the largest egg of any bird with eggs measuring up to eight inches (20 cm) long. Ostriches live in Africa. Because the ostrich is up to nine feet tall, it can see a long distance which helps the bird spot danger.

Several other flightless birds are related to the ostrich. The rhea looks much like a small ostrich. It grows up to five feet (1.5 m) tall. It lives on the plains of South America. The emu lives in Australia and also looks very much like an ostrich but is only about six feet (1.8 m) tall. Another large flightless bird somewhat resembling an ostrich is the cassowary, which also reaches heights of about six feet. The ostrich, rhea, and emu all have primarily gray or brown feathers. The cassowary is mostly black, but has a bright red and blue neck and head. The cassowary also has a large bony shield on its head called a **casque**. Cassowaries live in New Guinea and northern Australia. It is likely that all of these birds came from the same ostrich "kind" that was on the Ark.

Cassowary

The kiwi is another flightless bird that lives in New Zealand. The kiwi is much smaller than the ostrich-type birds mentioned above. It is only about 20 inches (51 cm) long. It has a very long beak with nostrils on the end. The kiwi uses these nostrils to sniff out food, which often includes earthworms and other small animals. Although the kiwi is about the size of a chicken, it can lay an egg that is nearly four times the size of a chicken egg. A kiwi has long thin feathers that from a distance could be mistaken for hair.

Kiwi

A very different group of flightless birds is the penguins. There are many different species of penguins, but they all have some common characteristics. Penguins live along coastal areas and spend much of their time in the water. They have webbed feet and wings which work as flippers to propel the bird through the water. Penguins are only found in the southern hemisphere.

King penguin

Some penguins, such as the Galapagos penguin, live in tropical areas, primarily on tropical islands with few land predators. Other penguins, such as the emperor penguin, live in Antarctica and are able to survive very harsh conditions. The emperor penguin is the largest penguin reaching heights up to four feet (1.2 m) tall. The little blue penguin is the smallest penguin at only 12 inches (30 cm) high.

Some people say that flightless birds are evidence for evolution, that they evolved from ancestors that could have flown in the past, and that their useless wings are just leftovers. However, is this really proof for evolution? It is not.

The "uselessness" of their wings is open to debate. These flightless birds still have muscles that control their wings and use them for various purposes. Some birds frighten away enemies by charging at them and flapping their wings. Other birds use their wings to shelter their young. And a penguin's wings are anything but useless. Their wings help them swim very quickly and dive deeply into the ocean for food. So even though these birds' wings do not help them fly, they are not useless.

The Bird's Digestive System

They sure eat a lot

Lesson 10

How is a bird's digestive system different from yours?

Words to know:

crop

gizzard

esophagus

cloaca

Challenge words:

counter-current exchange

Beginners

Have you ever noticed that birds are almost always eating? They need lots of energy for flying. Birds do not have any teeth so they cannot chew up their food, but God has given birds a special digestive system that allows them to get the energy they need without teeth.

When birds swallow their food, it goes into a special sac called a **crop** where it is slowly released into the stomach. The food then goes through the **gizzard** which is very rough inside. The gizzard helps grind up the food. This is why birds can eat without teeth. After passing through the gizzard, the food goes through the small intestine and the nutrients are absorbed. Finally the waste leaves the bird's body. This digestive system works very well to give the bird lots of energy.

- **Why do birds spend most of their time eating?**
- **Do birds chew up their food?**
- **How does a bird's food get ground up?**

Have you ever noticed that when birds are not flying they are almost always eating? This is because flying requires a lot of energy. In addition, warm-blooded animals need a lot of food to keep their bodies at a constant temperature. God created birds with a special digestive system to help them be able to fly and regulate their temperature.

First, a bird's digestive system works very quickly. A bird can digest its food in as little as 30 minutes to 3 hours. The human body takes several hours to as much as two days to completely digest its food. Second, a bird's digestive system is very efficient at extracting the nutrients it needs.

Bird's Digestive System

This special digestive system helps birds have the necessary energy for flight.

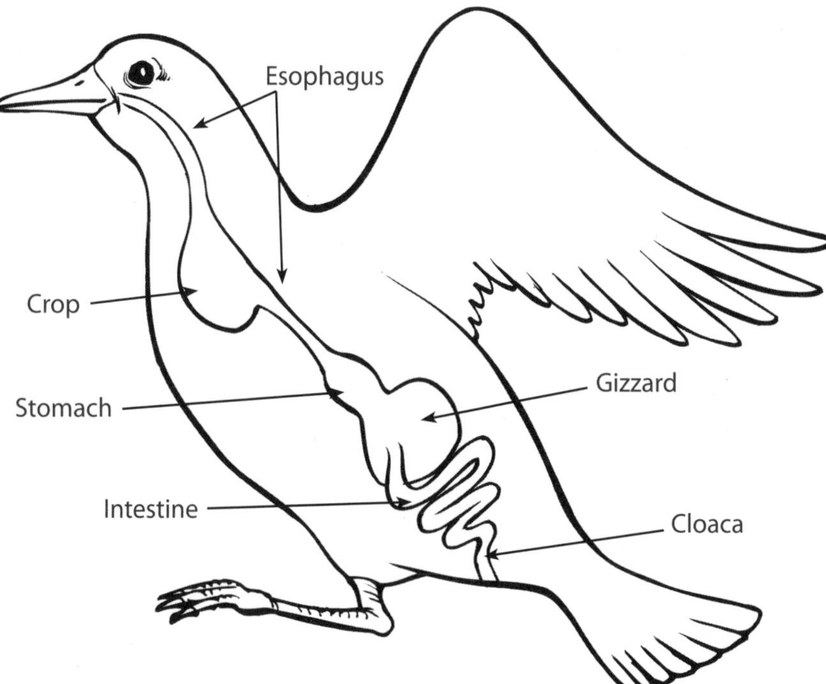

Birds do not have teeth, so God designed them with digestive systems that digest food that has not been chewed. A bird swallows its food, which enters its **esophagus**, the tube connecting the mouth to the stomach. The food is then held in a sac in the middle of the esophagus called a **crop**, to be released into the stomach at a constant rate. This allows a bird to eat quickly then fly to a safe place for digestion. The food then goes into a small stomach where digestive juices are added. The food then enters the **gizzard**. This organ is very rough inside and grinds up the food. The gizzard compensates for the bird's lack of teeth. After that, the food enters a small intestine where the nutrients are extracted, after which the waste goes through the **cloaca** to be eliminated. ■

Digestive system worksheet

Draw and label the parts of the bird's digestive system on the "God Designed the Bird's Digestive System" worksheet. This can be added to your animal notebook.

Dissect an owl pellet

Owl pellets can be ordered from many science supply stores. An owl swallows its prey whole and later spits up a pellet of indigestible fur and bones. You can obtain pellets that have been sterilized and dissect them to see what the owl had for dinner by matching the bones to a chart that can also be purchased. This is a fascinating project.

WHAT DID WE LEARN?

- How does a bird "chew" its food without teeth?
- What purposes does the crop serve?

TAKING IT FURTHER

- How is a bird's digestive system different from a human digestive system?
- How does a bird's digestive system help it to be a better flyer?

Respiratory system

God not only designed birds to have a special digestive system, He also designed them with a special respiratory system that allows them to get a higher percentage of oxygen out of the air than most other animals. This is a very efficient system, which allows birds to fly for extended periods of time without tiring, and enables them to fly at high altitudes where there is less oxygen in the air.

In most animals with lungs, including mammals and reptiles, the chest cavity expands drawing air into the lungs. The air passes through smaller and smaller passages in the lungs until it reaches tiny sacs that are surrounded by blood vessels. Oxygen passes into the blood and carbon dioxide leaves the blood and enters the air in these sacs. The chest cavity then compresses, forcing the air out of the lungs. This is a bellows type of process.

The bird's respiratory system is very different, however. The bird's lungs do not expand and contract. When a bird inhales, the air passes through the lungs into rear air sacs. As the bird exhales, the air passes through small tubes in the lungs where the exchange of oxygen takes place. When the bird inhales again, the air in these tubes is forced into forward air sacs. Finally when the bird exhales again the air in the forward air sacs leaves its body. Thus the bird inhales and exhales twice for each breath of air.

The blood flow through the lungs is in the opposite direction as the air flow. Blood is always exposed to air that has a higher concentration of oxygen. Thus, this opposite flow allows for the greatest amount of oxygen to be exchanged within the lungs. This is called **counter-current exchange**.

In addition to being very efficient in exchanging oxygen, the bird's respiratory system also serves another vital function. Air flowing through the air sacs also flows through small tubes inside the hollow spaces in the bird's bones. This removes heat from the bird's body as the cool air moves through the sac and out of the body again. This is a very efficient way to cool the bird while it is flying for long periods of time.

Earlier we examined some of the ways that birds are different from reptiles. Their respiratory system is one of the biggest differences. It is impossible to conceive of a way that the bellows type of respiratory system of a reptile could slowly change into the counter-current exchange system of a bird with slow gradual changes proposed by evolution. Again, we see that God created the different kinds the way they are for His glory.

Bottom view of bird's respiratory system

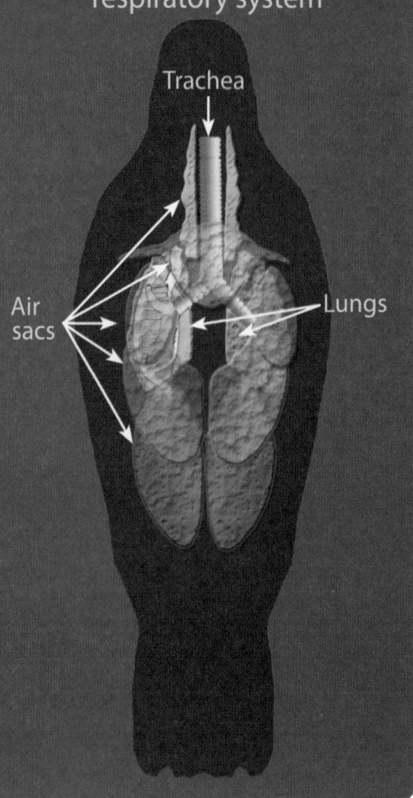

Fish

Do fish go to school?

LESSON 11

What features allow fish to survive underwater?

Words to know:

cold-blooded

gills

Beginners

Fish are very different animals from mammals and birds. They are different in many ways. First, fish always live in the water. Birds and most mammals live on the land. Mammals have hair and birds have feathers, but fish have scales covering their bodies.

Mammals and birds are both warm-blooded animals, but fish are **cold-blooded**. This means that the fish's body is the same temperature as the water that it is in. When the water is warm, the fish's body temperature is warm, but in the winter, when the water is near freezing, the fish's body temperature will also be near freezing.

Fish do not breathe air like mammals and birds. Instead, fish get oxygen from the water. Water flows through a fish's mouth and across its **gills**. The oxygen goes from the water into the fish through its gills. Most fish lay eggs, but a few fish give birth to live young.

- **Where do fish live?**
- **What do fish have covering their bodies?**
- **Are fish warm-blooded or cold-blooded?**
- **How do fish breathe?**
- **How do most fish reproduce?**

One of America's favorite pastimes is fishing. Fish can be found in the smallest ponds and streams, in large lakes, and throughout the oceans. There are over 22,000 species of fish, making them the most diverse group of vertebrates. Fish are vertebrates that live in the water. They have scales and they breathe oxygen from the water using **gills**, special organs that remove oxygen from the water. Fish are **cold-blooded**, which means that their bodies do not stay the same temperature all the time, but become the same temperature as their surroundings. This allows them to survive even in very cold climates. Most fish reproduce by laying eggs, although a few give live birth. Most fish live in either salt water or fresh water, but a few can survive in both salt and fresh water environments.

Fish breathe using their gills.

Most fish are bony fish, meaning they have bony skeletons. Bony fish have fins and tails that make them excellent swimmers. When you think of a fish, you probably think of a trout, bass, or goldfish. But about 5% of all fish do not have rigid bones. Instead, they have flexible skeletons made from cartilage. Cartilaginous fish include sharks, rays, and lampreys.

Even though dolphins and whales appear to be a lot like fish, recall that there are a few very impor-

Fish School

A group of fish is called a school just like a group of birds is called a flock. Create an underwater picture. Try to include seaweed, sand, rocks, or other sea life. Then glue a group of goldfish snack crackers on the picture to show a school of fish. Take a picture of your creation to include in your animal notebook. It can also be fun to eat some of the fish.

Name a Group Game

Have one person name an animal, then have another name what a group of that type of animal would be called. Here are a few to get you started: A school of fish, a flock of birds, a gaggle of geese, a herd of elephants, a pride of lions, a pack of wild dogs, a flock of sheep, a brood of vipers, a swarm of flies. (For a large list, go to www.infoplease.com/ipa/A0004725.html.)

Birds & Fish

tant differences. One of the most distinct differences is in how they breathe. As we already learned, dolphins, whales, and other aquatic mammals must periodically go to the surface for fresh air, which they take into their lungs. Fish, on the other hand, get their oxygen from the water. Water enters the fish's mouth, is forced over the gills, and then exits the fish's body. As the water passes over the gills, oxygen moves from the water into the fish's blood stream.

If a fish swims with its mouth open, there is a constant flow of water through the gills. If a fish is not swimming, it can force the water through the gills by contracting its throat. Some sharks cannot do this so they must continually stay in motion. ■

FUN FACT

Aquarium fish are the most popular pet in America, with nearly 12 million households owning more than 158,600,000 fish.

Birds & Fish

WHAT DID WE LEARN?

- What makes fish different from other animals?
- How do fish breathe?
- Why do some sharks have to stay in motion?
- What is the difference between warm-blooded and cold-blooded animals?

TAKING IT FURTHER

- Other than how they breathe, how are dolphins different from fish?
- How are dolphins like fish?

DESIGNED FOR WATER

Fish have been specially designed by God to survive in their watery environment. Do some research and find out how each of the following fish features specially equips the fish for living in the water. Write a short report to include in your animal notebook.

- Shape (some fish are flattened side to side; some fish are flattened top to bottom; some fish are snake-shaped)
- Scales
- Color
- Gills
- Eyes
- Swim bladders

Fins & Other Fish Anatomy

Designed for efficiency

Lesson 12

How are fins used by fish?

Words to know:

swim bladder

pectoral fin

pelvic fin

dorsal fin

anal fin

caudal fin

Challenge words:

olfactory lobe

lateral line

optic lobe

Beginners

Fish were designed to be good swimmers. They have long narrow bodies that move smoothly through the water. Their bodies produce a slimy liquid that makes them move even more easily through the water. Have you every tried to pick up a fish? It is very slippery and hard to hold on to.

Fish also have fins that help them swim. The fins near the front of their bodies help them to angle up or down in the water. These fins can also work as brakes to slow the fish down when it is swimming.

The fins on the top of the fish and near the back of the fish help to keep the fish from tipping sideways. And the tail fin helps to push the fish forward through the water. The fish has strong muscles all along its body to help it swim. The fish was created by God to be a great swimmer.

- **What is special about a fish body that helps it be a good swimmer?**
- **How do the front fins help the fish?**
- **How do the top and back fins help the fish?**
- **How does the tail help the fish?**

Most fish have a similar body shape that is long, thin, and somewhat flat. God designed a fish's body to be very efficient in the water. First, gills are designed to remove up to 80% of the oxygen from the water. By comparison, lungs usually remove only about 25% of the oxygen from the air.

To be efficient swimmers, God designed fish with long narrow bodies that glide easily through the water. The fish's body produces slimy mucus that coats the body and helps it swim more easily. To stay afloat, most fish have **swim bladders**. These are balloon-like sacs that can be inflated with air to help the fish rise in the water, or can be deflated to help the fish sink or go deeper in the water.

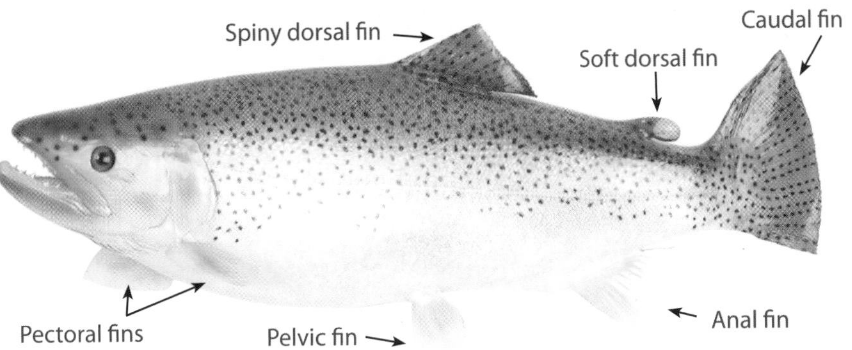

Finally, fish were designed with several different fins to help them be great swimmers. Fish have two pairs of fins toward the front of their bodies. **Pectoral fins** are located on the sides behind the mouth. The **pelvic fins** are lower down on the body. Pectoral and pelvic fins allow the fish to angle up or down when swimming. They can also act as brakes to slow the fish down. And they can even be used to slowly move the fish backward. These fins also help the fish swim in a straight line.

Fish usually have one or two fins that stick up on their backs. These are called **dorsal fins**. They also have a fin pointing down from the bottom called an **anal fin**. Dorsal and anal fins keep the fish from tipping sideways and give it stability.

The final fin is the tail, called the **caudal fin**. This is also called the tail fin. It provides the main power for forward movement in fish.

All of these designs, along with strong muscles, make the fish one of the most efficient swimmers in creation. God's great design is very evident in the fish's body.

One of the few exceptions to the fast-swimming fish is the seahorse. This tiny creature may not even seem like a fish, but it is cold-blooded, has fins, scales and gills, and lays eggs like other fish. This tiny fish has a dorsal fin that moves it forward in an upright position at a rather slow speed. However, just because it is slow does not mean it was not well designed.

A protective bony armor cleverly protects the seahorse from imminent danger. Its tough skeleton makes it unappetizing for predators, so sea horses are usually left alone.

The seahorse is unique among fishes in that its head is set at right angles to its body. It swims with its body held upright. It can bend its head down or up, but not from side to side. The inability to move its head from side to side would create problems in other creatures, but God in His wisdom has designed the seahorse's eyes to move independently, swiveling about to watch each side. ■

Fish fins worksheet

Cut fins from construction paper and glue them in the correct places on the "Fish Fins" worksheet. Label the fins and color the fish. This page can be included in your animal notebook.

WHAT DID WE LEARN?

- What is the purpose of a swim bladder?
- How did God design the fish to be such a good swimmer?

TAKING IT FURTHER

- How does mucus make a fish a more efficient swimmer?
- How has man used the idea of a swim bladder in his inventions?
- What other function can fins have besides helping with swimming?
- What similar design did God give to both fish and birds to help them get where they are going?

Nervous system

Fish are designed with an amazing nervous system. It is similar to the nervous system of other vertebrates in many ways, but in other ways it is very different. Like all vertebrates, a fish has a brain that is connected to a spinal cord and a series of nerves throughout its body. However, a fish can sense things that mammals cannot.

Most fish have a highly developed sense of smell and can find their food by smelling the water. The section of the brain responsible for smell is the **olfactory lobe**; this is one of the largest parts of the fish brain. This sense of smell also helps them sense predators in the area. Pacific salmon have such a good sense of smell that they can find their way from the ocean to the stream in which they hatched. It is believed that they can sense the smell of the particular water plants in that area or the soil run-off from the streams and these scents help to guide them home when it is time for them to reproduce.

Fish are very sensitive to even slight changes in ocean currents because of their lateral line. The **lateral line** is a series of special nerves that cover the head and sides of the fish. These nerve endings are protected by a row of pitted scales. The lateral line allows the fish to detect very low frequency vibrations, changes in pressure, and even slight turbulence in the water.

Sight is also very important to fish. The **optic lobes**, the parts of the brain responsible for sight, are often larger than the cerebrum and cerebellum combined. In proportion to its brain, a fish's eyes are quite large. Thus fish generally have very good eyesight.

Finally, fish can often sense things that most other animals cannot. Some fish can sense the electrical fields that are generated by the nervous systems of other animals. This is how some fish find their prey. Other fish can sense magnetic fields. This allows fish to navigate using the earth's magnetic field. The nervous system of fish is a design marvel, given to them by their Creator.

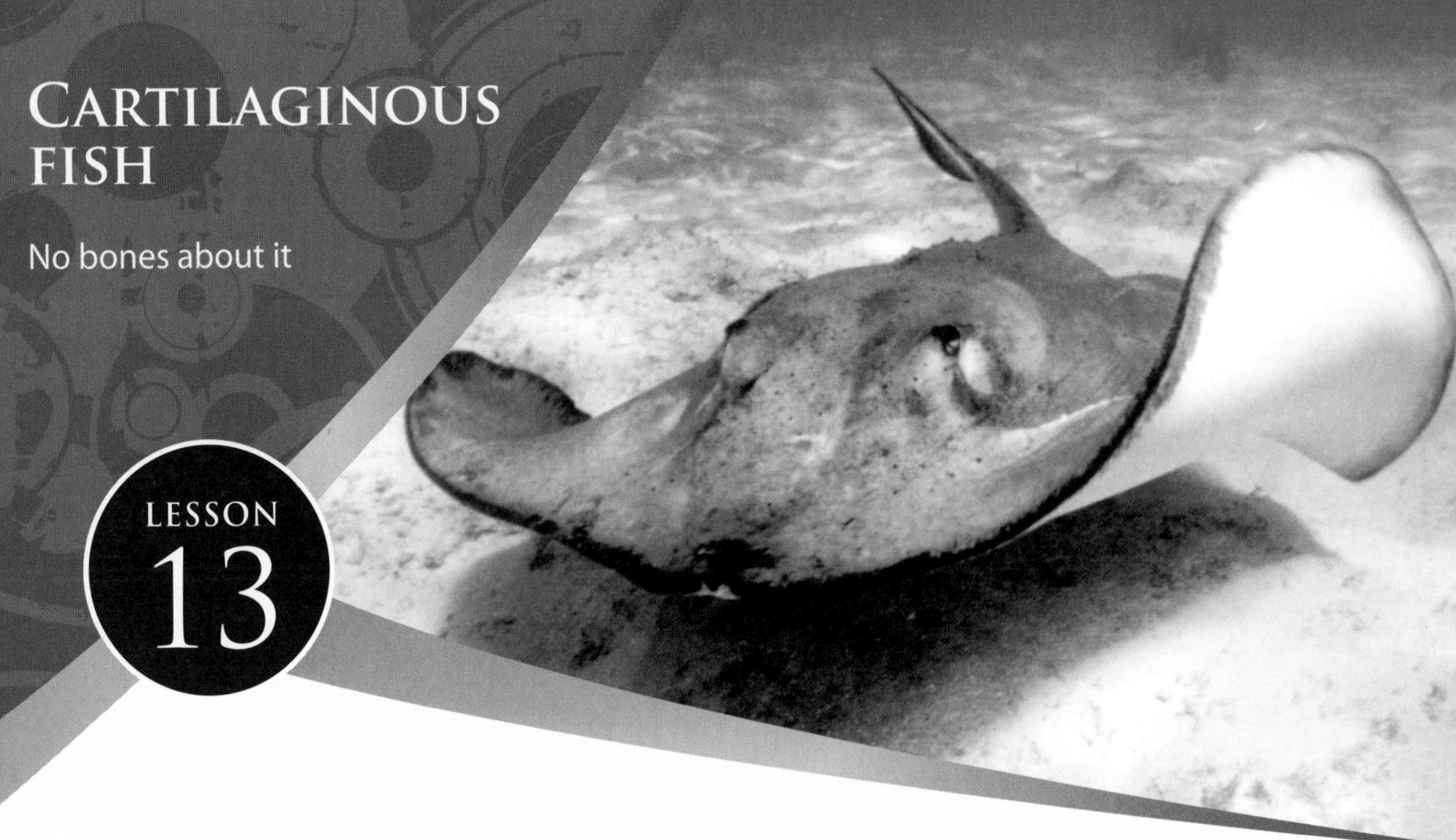

CARTILAGINOUS FISH

No bones about it

LESSON 13

What sets sharks apart from most other fish?

Words to know:

cartilage

parasite

scavenger

BEGINNERS

Most fish have bones inside their bodies, but a few have a flexible material called **cartilage** instead. Sharks and rays are two fish that don't have bones.

Sharks are shaped like most other fish. They are meat eaters, though the original shark kind was not. They catch their prey with their razor sharp teeth. Sharks are always growing new teeth. When one row of teeth wears out, a new row moves up to take its place. Many sharks give birth to live babies instead of laying eggs like most fish. When these babies are born, they are ready to take care of themselves and do not stay with the mother.

Rays (shown above) do not have the same shape as other fish. Instead, rays are wide and flat. They glide through the water using their fins like wings. Many rays are harmless to humans, but stingrays can give you a very painful, and sometimes deadly, sting with their tails.

- **How is a shark's skeleton different from other fish skeletons?**
- **What happens when a shark's teeth wear out?**
- **How does a ray use its fins to swim?**

About 5% of all fish do not have bony skeletons. These fish have cartilage structures instead. **Cartilage** is a tough yet flexible material that provides shape and structure without being stiff. Cartilage is what gives your nose and ears their shape. The most well-known cartilaginous fish is the shark. These fearsome fish can be as small as 6 inches (15 cm) or as big as 50 feet (15 m) long.

Like all animals, sharks were originally created to eat plant material, but today they are meat eaters. They can be found in most parts of the ocean. Most sharks have several rows of razor-sharp teeth. When one row of teeth wears out, the next row moves up to take its place.

Most sharks have the same general shape as the bony fish. However, their internal structure and function are quite different. First, sharks do not have swim bladders. If sharks quit swimming, they sink to the ocean floor. Also, many sharks cannot force water out of their throats, so they must remain in constant motion to keep water flowing over their gills. Sharks do not have covers over their gills. Instead, they have several gill slits that are easily visible on the sides of their bodies. Finally, many sharks give birth to live young instead of laying eggs.

Shark babies are born ready to care for themselves and leave their mothers right away. Sharks that lay eggs usually place their eggs in a thick egg sac and then never return. The young are on their own when they hatch.

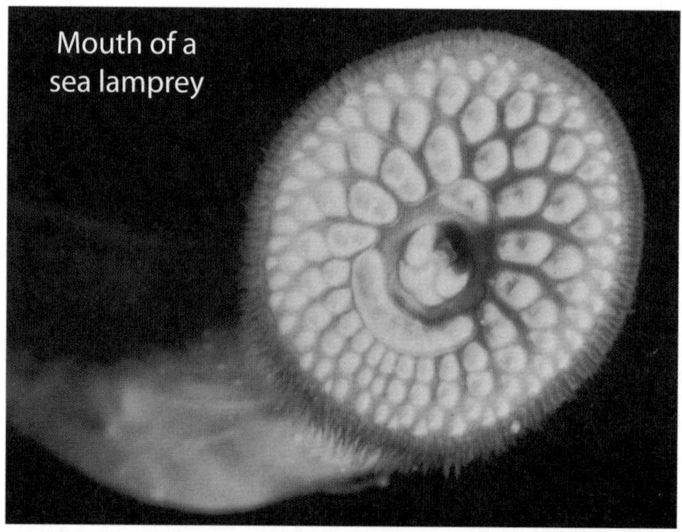
Mouth of a sea lamprey

Another type of cartilaginous fish is the ray (pictured at the beginning of this lesson). Rays do not have slim, tapered bodies; instead, they are wide and flat. They glide through the water using their pectoral fins like wings. Rays are generally harmless to man—except for the stingray. The stingray has a whip-like tail that can inject venom into its enemies or cause a painful sting and sometimes death in humans.

Other cartilaginous fish that are not shaped like most fish are the lampreys and hagfish. These fish resemble snakes with their long round bodies. They do not have

Clay Models

Use modeling clay to make models of cartilaginous fish such as sharks and rays. When you are done, take pictures to put in your animal notebook.

Birds & Fish

jaws like other fish. Instead, they have a sucking type of mouth (see photo on previous page). Lampreys are **parasites**—animals that take nutrients from a living host, often harming the host. They attach themselves to other fish and suck nutrients from their bodies. Lampreys are similar to eels. However, eels have bony skeletons and jaws, while lampreys have cartilaginous skeletons and no jaws. Hagfish are generally **scavengers**—animals that eat dead plants or animals. ■

WHAT DID WE LEARN?

- How do cartilaginous fish differ from bony fish?
- Why is a lamprey called a parasite?
- Why can sharks and stingrays be dangerous to humans?

TAKING IT FURTHER

- Why are shark babies born independent?
- What do you think is the shark's biggest natural enemy?

PICTURES OF CARTILAGINOUS FISH

There are over 600 species of cartilaginous fish. Collect as many pictures of cartilaginous fish as you can find. Put them together with descriptions of the fish and add them to your animal notebook. If you cannot find pictures to put in your notebook, paint or draw a picture of some of your favorite sharks and rays and put your drawings in your notebook.

UNIT 3

AMPHIBIANS & REPTILES

KEY CONCEPTS

- **Describe** the unique characteristics of reptiles and amphibians using examples.
- **Distinguish** between reptilian and amphibian life cycles.
- **Describe** how reptiles defend themselves.

UNIT LESSONS

Amphibians

Air or water?

Lesson 14

Which animals are classified as amphibians?

Words to know:

amphibian

larval stage

Beginners

Have you ever heard of an amphibian? How about a frog? A frog is an amphibian. **Amphibians** are animals that start out living in the water and breathing with gills. Then they change as they grow up. They develop lungs so they can breathe air, and many of them leave the water to live on land. But even the adults usually stay near water to keep their skin moist.

Amphibians are cold-blooded so their body temperature is the same as the temperature of their surroundings. Amphibians lay eggs to reproduce.

Frogs are not the only amphibians. Toads and salamanders are also amphibians. All of these animals look very different as babies than they do as adults. So you might not even recognize a baby salamander if you saw one.

- **Name three kinds of animals that are amphibians.**
- **How does an amphibian breathe as a baby?**
- **How does an amphibian breathe as an adult?**

Poison dart frog

As we have learned, there are five groups of vertebrates (animals with backbones). The first two groups we studied, mammals and birds, are warm-blooded. Their body temperature remains constant. The others—amphibians, reptiles, and fish—are cold-blooded. This means their body temperature goes up when the temperature around them is warm and down when their environment gets colder.

Amphibians are cold-blooded animals that have smooth moist skin. They generally live in very moist areas or near the water to keep their skin from drying out. They lay eggs. But the unique thing about amphibians is that they spend the first part of their lives in the water using gills to breathe. Then their bodies change and they develop lungs that allow them to breathe air. The word amphibian means "on both sides of life," reflecting this change.

The three major groups of amphibians are frogs and toads, salamanders, and caecilians (seh-SILL-yen). The vast majority of amphibians are frogs and toads. Frogs and toads come in many sizes and colors. Frogs usually have smooth moist skin and toads usually have more dry bumpy skin. Aquatic frogs live in or near the water. Many tree frogs live in the trees in tropical forests. Tree frogs are usually much more colorful and are often poisonous. Tree frogs also have suction cups on the bottoms of their feet to allow them to climb trees very quickly. Toads often live farther from the water but most must return to the water to reproduce.

Fun Fact

Many frogs can breathe not only with their lungs, but also through their skin. A frog's skin is thin and contains many mucous glands that keep it moist. Oxygen can be absorbed through this thin, damp skin.

Warm-blooded/Cold-blooded

Have one child pretend to be a warm-blooded animal such as a dog and have another child pretend to be a cold-blooded animal such as a frog. Act out what your animal might be doing if the temperature around you was 15°F (–9.4°C). Remember that cold-blooded animals cannot be active in cold weather and they often go into hibernation.

Now act out what your animals might do if the temperature was 65°F (18.3°C), and again if the temperature was 95°F (35°C). Remember that warm-blooded animals must find ways to keep their bodies warm in the cold weather and cool in the hot weather. Also remember that cold-blooded animals must find shade when the weather is too hot or sunshine when it is too cold.

A salamander

Salamanders have long thin bodies and tails. They might be confused with lizards, but their skin is smooth and moist, unlike a lizard's skin, which is dry and scaly. Also, as babies, salamanders look very different from lizards. They spend the first part of their lives in the water in a **larval stage**, an immature form, before they change into the more familiar adult form.

The smallest group of amphibians is the caecilians. Caecilians are legless amphibians that resemble worms. They are long and thin and usually burrow in the ground. Caecilians live in the tropical forests of South America, Africa, and Southeast Asia. Because they spend most of their lives underground, people seldom see them. ■

WHAT DID WE LEARN?

- What are the characteristics that make amphibians unique?
- How can you tell a frog from a toad?
- How can you tell a salamander from a lizard?

TAKING IT FURTHER

- What advantages do cold-blooded animals have over warm-blooded animals?
- What advantages do warm-blooded animals have over cold-blooded animals?
- Why are most people unfamiliar with caecilians?

ANIMAL COMMUNICATION

Animals communicate with each other in many different ways and for many different reasons. Animals communicate to find a mate, to mark and protect their territory, and to warn enemies or predators to stay away. Animals use sounds, body markings, and chemicals to communicate.

Amphibians primarily communicate by sound. You have probably heard frogs and toads croaking on a warm summer evening. Male frogs and toads have inflatable air sacs or throat pouches that help amplify their calls. This allows them to talk to others of their species, primarily to find a mate.

But their communication goes far beyond simple croaking. Every species has a different call with a different frequency that it uses for communication. A female bullfrog for instance will only respond to a call from a male bullfrog. She will ignore calls from tree frogs or other types of frogs. In tests, a frog could distinguish between the calls of 35 different types of frogs and only responded to calls from the same species. Not only does each species produce a unique sound, but many species have ears that are particularly tuned to the call of their species. They have selective hearing.

There may be many species of frogs and toads living in a particular area, especially in rainforests or jungles. In order to make their communication more clear, these amphibians do more than

Amphibians & Reptiles

just use different frequencies to communicate. Some amphibians use "time sharing," that is, certain species communicate only at particular times of the day or night. Frogs are also able to detect how often other frogs are croaking and time their croaks to be in between other croaks so they can be heard. Some species also increase their volume so that they can be heard above other species. One species of frog can make noises that are so loud they are near the pain threshold for humans.

Although amphibians primarily communicate by sound, they can also communicate in other ways. One unmistakable way that poison dart frogs communicate with their predators is with their bright colors. These brilliantly-colored amphibians produce a toxic chemical on their skin. Their bright colors warn predators to stay away. Natives to Central and South America where these frogs live have learned to imitate the calls of the poison dart frogs to capture them. They then collect the poison from the frogs' skins and dip their arrows in the poison. These arrows are then used for hunting. The poison instantly paralyzes a deer or other animal shot with the arrow. The poison is only effective when it enters the blood stream. It is broken down in the digestive system so the hunter can eat the animal without fear of poisoning himself.

Look for other ways that animals communicate with each other. Look for patterns on their bodies, listen to the noises they make, and even smell the scents they leave behind. These are all ways that animals talk to each other. For fun, get three friends or siblings together and try to practice communicating the way frogs do. Have one person make a short noise every second. Have a second person make a different noise in between the first person's noises. Then you try to carry on a conversation with a third person. The trick is that you and your partner can only talk when both of the other people are quiet. This is very difficult to do. Does this help you appreciate how well God designed frogs to communicate with each other?

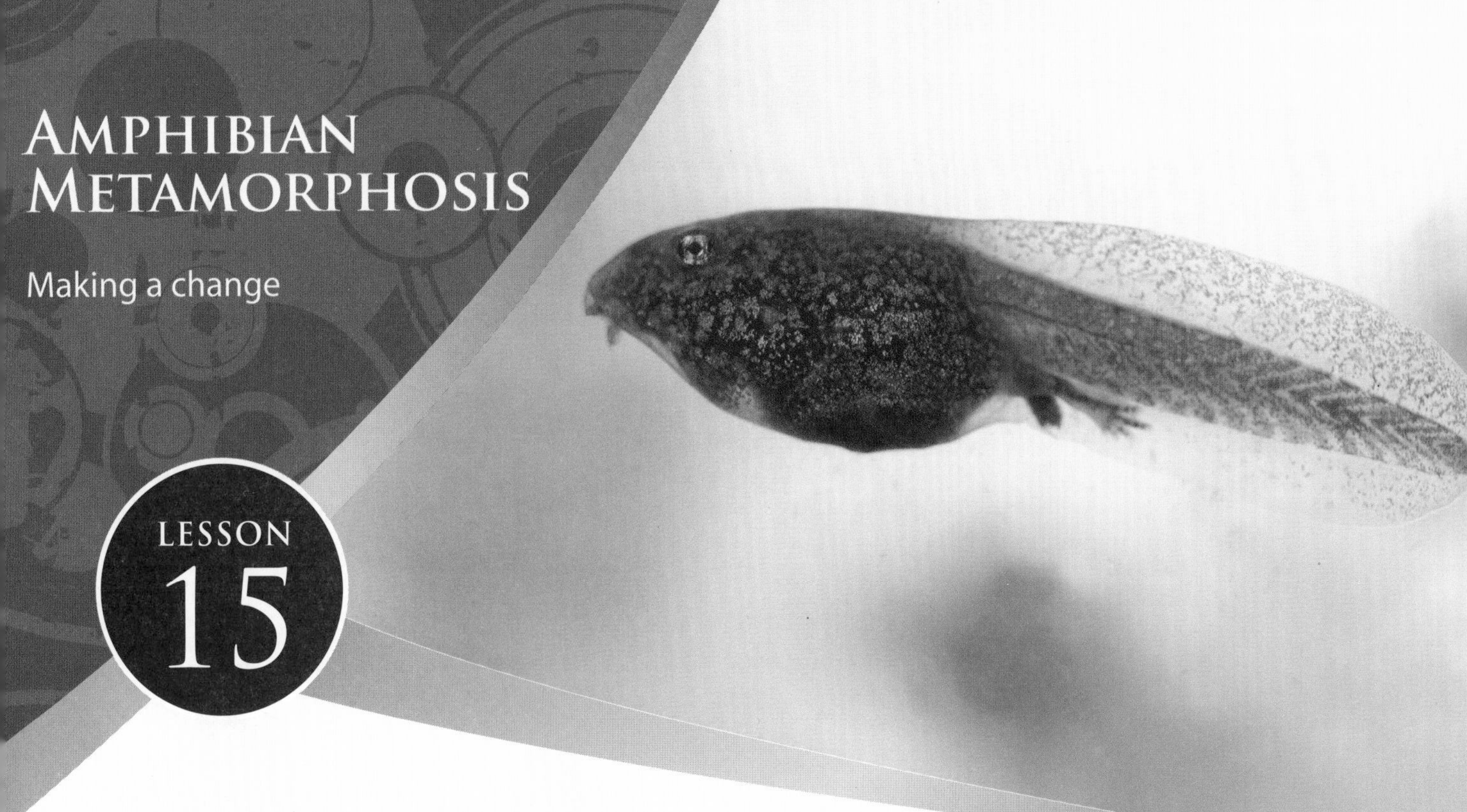

Amphibian Metamorphosis

Making a change

Lesson 15

What changes happen in metamorphosis?

Words to know:

metamorphosis

tadpole

pollywog

Beginners

Some baby animals look very much like their parents when they are born, but frogs and other amphibians do not look anything like their parents when they are born. A frog starts out as an egg that has been laid in the water. What hatches out of the egg is a **tadpole** that looks a little bit like a tiny fish. The tadpole swims around in the water and eats and grows. It breathes water through its gills.

As the tadpole grows, its body begins to change. Legs begin to grow and its tail begins to shrink. At the same time, the tadpole begins to develop lungs. When the frog is fully grown it looks like its parents. It no longer breathes water, but breathes air instead. It is now ready to leave the water and live on land. The frog will someday return to the water to lay eggs and start the life cycle over again.

- **What is a baby frog called?**
- **What does a tadpole look like?**
- **How does a tadpole change as it grows?**

Amphibians do what no other animals do. They start out in life using gills to get oxygen from water. Then they slowly change into an adult with lungs to get oxygen from the air. The most familiar amphibian is the frog. Although most amphibians go through this **metamorphosis**, or change, we will examine the changes a frog experiences to better understand this process.

Most frogs go to the water to reproduce, even if they do not live in or near the water the rest of the time. Their eggs are laid in a mass in the water. A jelly-like substance coats and protects the eggs until they hatch. Eggs usually hatch in 6–9 days.

What hatches from the egg is called a **tadpole** (or sometimes a **pollywog**). The tadpole is the larval stage in the frog's life cycle. This "infant" frog has a tail for swimming and looks a little like a small fish. It lives in the water and spends most of its time eating and growing. The tadpole has gills, which are organs that transfer oxygen from the water into the animal's blood stream.

In a matter of weeks, the tadpole begins to change noticeably. This change is called metamorphosis. During metamorphosis,

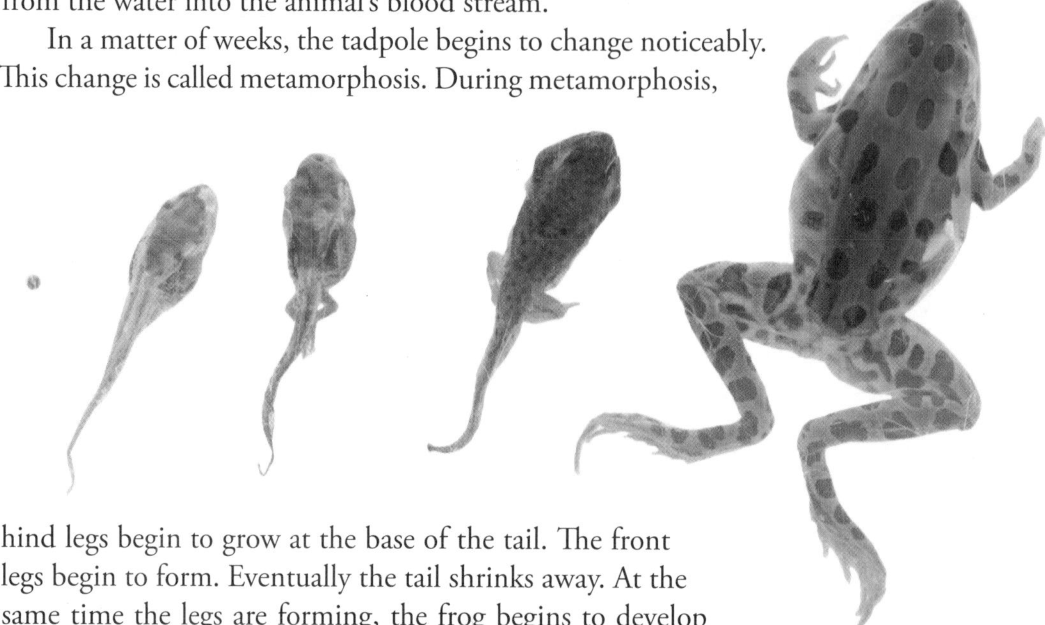

hind legs begin to grow at the base of the tail. The front legs begin to form. Eventually the tail shrinks away. At the same time the legs are forming, the frog begins to develop lungs. Lungs are organs that transfer oxygen from the air to

Amphibian Life Cycle

After looking at pictures of a frog changing from a tadpole into an adult, draw a picture representing each stage of an amphibian's life cycle on the "Amphibian Life cycle" worksheet. Add this sheet to your animal notebook.

Optional—Grow a Frog

The best way to appreciate the metamorphosis of a frog is to get a tadpole and watch it change day by day. Science supply catalogs often sell kits that come with a live tadpole and pet stores sometimes sell tadpoles. Or if you live near a pond, you might be able to catch some tadpoles to raise and then release the grown frogs.

the animal's bloodstream. Until the lungs are fully developed, the frog uses gills to extract oxygen from the water. Once the lungs are ready, the gills begin to disappear and the tadpole has transformed into a frog! Most adult frogs leave the water and spend the majority of their adult lives on land and return to the water only to lay eggs. A few types of frogs continue to live close to the water throughout their lives. This transformation from a water-dweller with gills to a land-dweller with lungs is what makes amphibians unique. ■

WHAT DID WE LEARN?

- Describe the stages an amphibian goes through in its life cycle.
- What are gills?
- What are lungs?

TAKING IT FURTHER

- Does the amphibian life cycle represent molecules-to-man evolution? Why or why not?

Amphibians & Reptiles

UNUSUAL AMPHIBIANS

Most amphibians lay their eggs in water where the tadpoles hatch and then grow into adults. However, some amphibians have unusual methods of reproduction. Some amphibians experience metamorphosis inside the egg; the tadpole changes from a water-breathing creature into an air-breathing creature before it hatches. It emerges from the egg looking like a miniature adult. A few species of salamanders and caecilians give birth to live young.

Some amphibians do not complete metamorphosis unless they experience unusual stress in their environments. The axolotl is a salamander that lives in lakes near Mexico City. It often remains in the tadpole stage its whole life and only develops into the adult form under unusual circumstances. It can reproduce by laying eggs while it is a tadpole.

The Surinam toad has a very interesting breeding process. The female lays eggs, then after fertilizing the eggs, the male uses his body to press them into the spongy skin on the female's back. The eggs hatch but the young tadpoles stay inside the skin on the mother's back until they change into fully formed toads. Then the tiny toads emerge from their mother's back, ready for life on their own.

Mouth-brooding frogs have an even more interesting method for raising their young. The female lays the eggs and the male fertilizes them. Then, as the eggs are beginning to hatch, the male swallows the eggs and keeps them in his voice sac. There the tadpoles eat their own egg yolks and begin to develop. After about three weeks the tadpoles have transformed into frogs and the father spits them out into the water where they begin their independent lives.

Another father that plays an unusual role in the reproduction process is the midwife toad. The female lays her eggs on land. The male then fertilizes the eggs and wraps them around his hind legs. For about a month, the father carries the eggs around and frequently dips them in the water to keep them moist. After about a month, the eggs are ready to hatch and the father lowers them into shallow water and removes them from his legs. The tadpoles stay in the water until they complete metamorphosis, then they leave the water and live primarily on land.

Look at an animal encyclopedia or other source to find out about other unusual methods of amphibian reproduction. Although the methods may differ, they all still go through the stages of metamorphosis.

REPTILES

Scaly animals

LESSON 16

Where are scales found on reptiles?

Words to know:

nictitating membrane

hibernation

Challenge words:

ceratopsian

plated dinosaur

theropod

sauropod

BEGINNERS

Do you know what a reptile is? You probably know about some animals that are reptiles. Lizards, snakes, and turtles are all reptiles. Crocodiles and alligators are reptiles, too. Dinosaurs are reptiles that we know only from fossils. Some people like reptiles, but other people don't like them at all.

Reptiles are cold-blooded animals. Reptiles have lungs and breathe air, and most reptiles lay eggs. They also have scales on their skin. Some reptiles, like snakes, have scales all over. Other reptiles, like turtles, only have scales on their legs, necks, and tails.

Reptiles can be found in all parts of the world. Many reptiles that live in warm areas are awake at night and sleep during the day. Those that live in very cold areas often **hibernate** or sleep during the coldest parts of the winter.

- **Name three different kinds of reptiles.**
- **What do reptiles have covering their skin?**
- **Where do reptiles live?**

Ever since the serpent tempted Eve in the garden of Eden, reptiles have held a strange fascination and often fear for humans. Reptiles are vertebrates with dry, scaly skin. Most lay eggs (though some bear live young), breathe with lungs, and are cold-blooded. Most reptiles have clear eyelids called **nictitating membranes** that cover and protect their eyes. These membranes are needed so the animal can still see even if it is in harsh conditions such as in a desert windstorm or underwater.

Fun Fact

Since cold-blooded animals don't burn energy to heat their bodies, reptiles eat 30 to 50 times less food than do birds and mammals (warm-blooded animals) of similar sizes.

The four major groups of reptiles are snakes, lizards, turtles, and crocodiles. In addition to these, there is one species of tuatara. Tuataras are similar to lizards but have a slower metabolism, a different bone structure, and mate differently than lizards. Scientists call these creatures "living fossils" because they are similar to fossil tuataras and supposedly have not changed for more than 200 million years. Mutations (genetic copying mistakes) are happening all the time, yet if one believed these imaginary long ages, this creature has gone through maybe a billion or more generations virtually unchanged. In fact, there are hundreds of "living fossils" recognized today. For those who believe the Bible, however, there should be no mystery about these so-called "living fossils." We have an eyewitness account (God's Word) of how these creatures were created only a few thousand years ago to be fruitful and multiply after their kind. So the fact that modern creatures are similar to their fossilized ancestors is no surprise at all.

A tuatara

Fun Fact

Tuataras have a "third eye" on top of their heads, which cannot see, but is sensitive to light. Scientists are not sure of the function of this eye, but it may be for telling them when to hibernate, or for allowing young tuataras to soak up the sun to make vitamin D, giving them the nourishment they need to grow into mature adults.

Scaly Picture

Draw an outline of a reptile, and then glue sequins wherever the creature would have scales on its body. Turtles only have scales on their legs, feet, tail, neck, and head. Alligators have very large scales on their bodies. Snakes have scales over their entire bodies. Include this picture in your animal notebook.

Of the 6,800 different kinds of reptiles, about half are lizards. Another 2,700 species are snakes. There are only about 240 kinds of turtles and only 21 kinds of crocodiles and alligators.

Reptiles live in all parts of the world. Because they are cold-blooded, many reptiles in hot tropical climates are nocturnal so they can sleep during the hottest part of the day and hunt at night when it is cool. Reptiles can also live in very cold climates. But because their bodies slow down so much in the cold, they go into a sort of **hibernation**, a sort of sleep where the animal's body processes significantly slow down until the weather warms up. ■

WHAT DID WE LEARN?

- What makes reptiles different from amphibians?
- What are the four groups of reptiles?

TAKING IT FURTHER

- How do reptiles keep from overheating?
- What would a reptile likely do if you dug it out of its winter hibernation spot?

DINOSAURS

Although there is some controversy over whether dinosaurs should be considered reptiles, they were originally classified as reptiles so we will talk about them in this section. Since no known living dinosaurs have been found, everything we know about dinosaurs comes from fossil evidence, which is open to some interpretation, so there are disputes and disagreements about many aspects of dinosaurs. However, there are many ideas that are commonly accepted among both creationists and evolutionists concerning dinosaurs.

Dinosaur fossils have been found all over the world from Alaska to Africa to Australia. Many dinosaurs were small. *Compsognathus* was the smallest known dinosaur at about 6 pounds (3 kg). It was probably about the size of a cat or a chicken. Other small dinosaurs include the *Podokesaurus*, which stood 3–5 feet (1–1.5 m) tall and the *Strithiomimus*, which was 6–8 feet (2– 2.4 m) tall. These small dinosaurs walked on two feet and ate small lizards, insects, and other small animals.

Another group of dinosaurs includes the horned dinosaurs called **ceratopsians.** *Triceratops* is probably the best known of the ceratopsians. These dinosaurs walked on all four legs and had massive skulls with various numbers

Chasmosaurus

of horns on their heads. God designed the horned dinosaurs' bodies to support their massive heads. The neck and shoulders of these animals are stronger than in other animals. Also, the first several vertebrae in their necks are fused together to help support the weight of the massive skull. Other horned dinosaurs include the *Torosaurus*, *Styracosaurus*, *Nonoclonius*, and the *Eucentrosaurus*.

Stegosaurus is one of the plated dinosaurs. **Plated dinosaurs** had rows of large plates down the sides of their backs. The grooves and spaces in the plate fossils suggest that there could have been significant blood flow through these plates. If this was true, the plates were likely used to cool the body of the dinosaur. Plated dinosaurs also have large spikes on their tails, which were likely used for self-defense. The *Kentrosaurus* and the *Tuojiangosaurus* were also plated dinosaurs.

Probably the most well known group of dinosaurs is **theropods**—meat-eating dinosaurs with large back legs and very small front legs. This group includes the *Tyrannosaurus rex* and the allosaurs. The *T. rex* is the largest known carnivore weighing in at 6 to 7 tons and measuring up to 50 feet (15 m) long. Its mouth was full of razor sharp teeth as long as a man's hand. The front arms of these meat eaters were short and not very strong.

The largest dinosaurs belong to the sauropod group of dinosaurs. **Sauropods** have long necks and tails and column-like legs. This group includes the *Diplodocus*, the *Apatosaurus*, and the *Brachiosaurus*. These massive animals were up to 100 feet (30 m) long. Some think they were able to rise up on their hind legs so they could reach branches high up in the trees. The sauropods likely spent much of their time in the water.

Many controversies rage over the interpretation of dinosaur fossils and what they tell us about these fascinating creatures. One of the biggest controversies is whether the dinosaurs were cold-blooded or warm-blooded animals. Do a search on the Answers in Genesis web site (www.answersingenesis.org) to see what the latest research has to say about this controversy.

Create one or more pages on dinosaurs for your notebook. Include any interesting information you find.

Special **FEATURE**

When Did the Dinosaurs Live?

When did dinosaurs live? If you listen to many scientists, they will tell you that dinosaurs lived from 230 million to 65 million years ago—long before man walked the earth. But you must remember that fossils don't come with labels telling how old they are. The idea of millions of years of evolution is just a story about the past.

The Bible, our source for truth, tells us that land animals (which would include dinosaurs) were created on the Day Six of Creation along with man about 6,000 years ago. God judged the world with a global Flood about 4,400 years ago, but representatives of all the kinds of air-breathing, land-dwelling animals survived on board the Ark with Noah and his family. What happened to the land animals that were not on board the Ark? They drowned. Most of the fossils around the earth today were formed as a result of the Flood. Therefore, most of the dinosaur fossils we find are about 4,400 years old, not millions of years.

Despite what some claim, there is abundant evidence that man and dinosaurs lived together:

- In Job 40:15–24, God describes to Job (who lived after the Flood) a great beast called *behemoth*. It is described as "the chief of the ways of God"—perhaps the largest land animal God created. Impressively, he moved his tail like a cedar tree! Although some Bible commentaries say this may have been an elephant or hippopotamus, the description actually fits that of a dinosaur like *Brachiosaurus*.
- Almost every culture has stories of dragons, and there are many very old history books in libraries around the world that have detailed records of dragons and their encounters with people. Surprisingly (or not so surprisingly for creationists), many of these descriptions of dragons fit how modern scientists would describe dinosaurs.
- In the North Atlantic during World War I, seconds after a German U-boat sunk the British steamer *Iberian*, there was an underwater explosion. The U-boat commander and some of his officers reported: "A little later pieces of wreckage, and among them a gigantic sea animal, writhing and strug-

gling wildly, were shot out of the water. . . . It was about 60 feet [18 m] long, was like a crocodile in shape and had four limbs with powerful webbed feet and a long tail tapering to a point."

- The tomb of Bishop Richard Bell in Carlisle Cathedral (UK) shows engravings of animals, including a fish, an eel, a dog, a pig, a bird, a weasel . . . and a dinosaur! This man died in 1496 and these brass engravings attest to the possible existence of dinosaurs only 500 years ago.
- The Ica stones of Peru were found in a cave that was exposed in the first half of the twentieth century by the flooding of the Ica River. The cave proved to be a repository of more than 15,000 carved stones. These artifacts from South America depict dinosaurs and flying reptiles of all types and sizes. This stone art is believed to date from 500–1000 AD.
- Over the past 100 years, there have been many reports of sightings, in a remote area of central Africa, of a swamp-dwelling animal known to local villagers as "mokele-mbembe"—the "blocker-of-rivers." It is described as living mainly in the water, its size somewhere between that of a hippopotamus and an elephant, but with a squat body and a long neck. The creature is said to climb the shore at daytime in search of food. Witnesses' drawings show that mokele-mbembe resembles nothing recognizable as alive on earth today, but it does bear a startling likeness to a sauropod dinosaur known to us by its fossil skeletons—similar in shape to a small *Apatosaurus*.
- Stories of giant man-eating birds (similar to pterosaurs) are common among many Indian tribes of the American Southwest. The Yaqui Indians spoke of a giant bird that lived on the hill of Otan Kawi. Every morning it would fly out to capture its human prey. After many deaths, a young boy who lost his family to this bird killed the creature with a bow and arrows.
- In Utah there is other evidence that suggests man lived with pterosaurs. In the Black Dragon Canyon, there is a beautiful pictograph of a pterosaur. The Indians of the Swell apparently saw a bird-like creature with enormous wings, a tail, a long neck, a beak, and a vertical head crest.
- In 2005 scientists from the University of Montana announced that they had found *T. rex* bones that were not totally fossilized. Interior sections of the bones were like fresh bone and contained soft tissue. If these bones really were millions of years old, this organic matter would have totally disintegrated.

So, what happened to the dinosaurs? If they were so big and powerful, why aren't they around today? After the Flood, the land animals, including dinosaurs, came off the Ark and lived alongside people. Because of sin, the judgments of the Fall and the Flood have greatly changed the earth. Post-Flood climatic change, lack of food, disease, and man's activities caused many types of animals to become extinct. The dinosaurs, like many other creatures, died out.

By looking at all the evidence, we see that it is explained by the biblical account that man and dinosaurs were created at the same time and lived together for much of history. For more information on dinosaurs, visit www.answersingenesis.org/go/dinosaurs.

Snakes

Those hissing, slithering creatures

LESSON 17

How do snakes move without any legs?

Words to know:

Jacobson's organ
constrictor
colubrid
venomous
lateral undulation
rectilinear movement
concertina movement
side winding

Beginners

Do you know what a snake looks like? It is long and thin and round. It is the most common reptile without legs. Snakes can be short or long and have eyes on the sides of their heads.

Snakes do not have to eat very often, only once every few days. Snakes eat lots of different things from eggs to mice and other small animals. A snake can eat animals that are larger than itself because its bottom jaw can be disconnected to allow its mouth to open very wide.

There are many different kinds of snakes. Most snakes are nonvenomous and are generally helpful for getting rid of mice and rats. Some common snakes are bull snakes, rat snakes, and garter snakes. Some snakes kill their food by wrapping their bodies around their prey and squeezing until the animal suffocates. These snakes are called **constrictors**. Pythons and boas are common constrictors.

A few snakes are **venomous** and should be avoided. These snakes can strike with their fangs and inject poison into their victims. Many venomous snakes are poisonous to animals but not to people; however, a few snakes are poisonous to people. Rattlesnakes, coral snakes, and cobras are some snakes that are poisonous to people.

- **What does a snake look like?**
- **How can a snake eat something bigger around than itself?**
- **Name three kinds of snakes.**

The vast majority of reptiles are snakes and lizards. Snakes are the most common legless reptiles. Snakes all have the same general shape—long and round—but can be as short as 5 inches (12.5cm) or as long as 30 feet (9 m).

Cobra

Snakes have eyes on the sides of their heads but no eyelids. Instead, they have clear scales that fit over their eyes. They do not have external ears. Instead, they sense vibrations and low noises through their lower jaw, which sends the vibration to an inner ear. Snakes have nostrils that help with smell but, in addition, each time they flick their tongues, they pick up scent particles. These particles are then touched to the **Jacobson's organ** in the top of the mouth. This organ is very sensitive to smell and allows the snake to follow the scent of its prey.

Snakes do not need to eat very frequently since they are cold-blooded. A warm-blooded animal eats frequently because it requires more energy to maintain its body temperature. Cold-blooded animals do not have to eat as often since they do not maintain a specific temperature—they do not need as much energy as a warm-blooded animal.

Coral snake

Snakes eat many different kinds of prey, from insects to large mammals, depending on the size of the snake. Snakes cannot chew or tear their food; instead, they swallow it whole. Snakes are able to do this because their lower jaws are not permanently attached to their skulls. They can disconnect their lower jaws and stretch their mouths around something much larger than the diameter of their own bodies. After swallowing its meal, the snake's strong muscles squeeze its prey as it begins digestion.

Boa constrictor

Most snakes fall into one of three groups: constrictors, colubrids, and venomous snakes. Constrictors are found mostly in tropical jungles. **Constrictors** overcome their prey by wrapping around and squeezing it. As the victim exhales, the constrictor squeezes tightly. After a few minutes, the prey has suffocated, and the snake then eats it. Pythons and boas are some of the most familiar constrictors.

Over two-thirds of all snakes are colubrids. **Colubrids** are found in most parts of the world. Most of these snakes are nonvenomous and many are useful for keeping down the rodent population. Bull snakes, rat snakes, and garter snakes are some common colubrids.

The most feared snakes are the **venomous** or poisonous snakes. These snakes have fangs that are used to inject venom into their prey. The venom attacks the nervous system, circulatory system, or both. The prey is usually paralyzed and

SLITHERING LIKE A SNAKE

Lie on the floor and try to move in the following ways. It may not be easy to match the movements of a snake, but you will have fun trying.

Snakes move in one of four ways.

1. Lateral undulation—Sideways waves

The most common way for a snake to move is in this S-shaped squiggling. The snake's body moves in curves from side to side. Snakes can move on land or in the water this way. Lie on your stomach, then try squiggling from side to side without using your arms.

2. Rectilinear—Straight line

Snakes that exhibit rectilinear movement stretch then contract their bodies in a straight line. They use their scales to help anchor one part of their bodies while they move another part. Lie on your stomach, pull your knees up to your chest and then stretch back out.

3. Concertina—Coiling

This is a slinky type of movement where the snake coils up then uncoils like a spring. Lie on your side, bend at the waist and knees, then push with your feet to spring forward.

4. Side winding—Angled

A sidewinder anchors its head and tail, moves its body sideways, and then moves its head and tail to match the body. The result is a diagonal movement to the direction the snake is facing. Lie on your stomach, move your hips sideways, move your head and shoulders to line up with your hips and then repeat this motion.

stops breathing in a matter of minutes. Then the snake can eat its meal without a struggle. Many venomous snakes, but not all, are poisonous to humans. Some well-known venomous snakes include rattlesnakes, coral snakes, and cobras.

For more on snakes, and how they fit into God's design, see www.answersingenesis.org/go/snakes. ■

WHAT DID WE LEARN?

- How are snakes different from other reptiles?
- What are the three groups of snakes?
- How is a snake's sense of smell different from that of most other animals?
- What is unique about how a snake eats?

TAKING IT FURTHER

- How are small snakes different from worms?
- If you see a snake in your yard, how do you know if it is dangerous?

SNAKE RESEARCH

There are over 2,300 species of snakes. We have only scratched the surface in this lesson. Use an animal encyclopedia or the Internet to find out more about snakes. Make a snake presentation to include in your animal notebook. Include pictures and interesting facts that you find about various kinds of snakes.

Special **FEATURE**

Rattlesnakes

It's a sound that puts fear in every heart: the gentle rattle coming from the grass. Rattlesnakes can be a frightening and dangerous sight. Yet, they are very interesting creatures. Rattlesnakes are the largest snakes that live in the United States. They can be found in nearly every part of North and South America.

Rattlesnakes are different from all other snakes because they have a rattle on the end of their tails. Each time a rattlesnake outgrows and sheds its old skin (a process called molting) its rattle gains another ring. These rings hitting each other as the snake shakes its tail are what give the rattlesnake its distinctive sound.

Rattlesnakes are vipers and are therefore venomous. They kill their prey by injecting it with venom. The snake bites its prey very quickly and then pulls back. The animal will run away but will soon die. The poison paralyzes the animal and then begins to break down its body before the snake even swallows it. The snake then uses its sense of smell to track down the animal and swallows it whole shortly after it dies.

Rattlesnakes seldom bite people. If someone approaches the snake, it usually gives a warning by shaking its tail to frighten them. If you should come upon a rattler, be sure to stay at least 10 feet (3 m) away. A snake can only strike about half the length of its body, so if you stay back it cannot bite you. A rattler will usually not bite someone unless that person persists in getting too close. Rattlers bite about one thousand people each year in the United States. Nearly everyone who is bitten survives if they go to a hospital for treatment. Doctors have developed a serum called antivenin (or antivenom), which is made from the venom of rattlesnakes and helps by breaking down the toxins in the venom.

Although rattlesnakes can be harmful to people, they can also be very helpful. Snakes are some of the best mice and rat hunters and are helpful in keeping down the pest population.

- There are 70 different kinds of rattlesnakes.

- A rattlesnake's rattle is made from keratin—the same material your fingernails are made of.
- Rattlesnakes hatch their young inside their bodies before giving birth.
- A rattlesnake can eat an animal as big as a five-pound (2.2 kg) rabbit.
- Rattlesnakes have no eyelids; in fact, no snakes have eyelids.
- The smallest adult rattlesnake is the pygmy rattlesnake, which grows to only 18 inches (46 cm) long.
- The largest rattlesnake is the Eastern diamondback, which grows up to 8 feet (2.4 m) long.
- The most poisonous rattlesnake in the United States is the Western diamondback.
- If a rattlesnake loses a fang, it can grow a new one.
- About 10 people die each year in the United States from rattlesnake bites.

Lizards

Chameleons and Gila monsters

LESSON 18

How do lizards protect themselves?

Beginners

Lizards have long thin bodies with legs that come out of the sides of their bodies. Lizards have tapered tails and their feet have claws. A lizard's body is covered with scales. Lizards can be found in nearly every part of the world.

A few lizards eat plants, but most lizards eat insects. People who live in tropical areas where there are many insects often keep pet lizards around to help eat the insects.

Lizards are very good at protecting themselves from their enemies. Lizards called chameleons can change the color of their bodies to match their surroundings. This makes the chameleon hard to see so it is less likely to be attacked. Some lizards are covered with spikes, which make them difficult to eat so they are often left alone. Sometimes, if an enemy grabs onto a lizard's tail, the tail will break off and the lizard will get away. The great part is that the lizard's tail will grow back. God made the lizards so that they can protect themselves from danger in this sin-cursed world.

- **What common body parts do all lizards have?**
- **What do most lizards eat?**
- **How does a chameleon protect itself from its enemies?**

Lizards are the largest group of reptiles. They have long thin bodies with legs that attach to the sides of their bodies. They have tapered tails. Their feet have claws, and they are covered with scales.

Lizards can be found in nearly every climate and ecosystem. They range in size from a few inches to 12 feet (3.7 m). Most lizards are not dangerous to humans, but the Gila monster is venomous, and Komodo dragons can cause infection if they bite a human.

Gila Monster

Lizards have various ways to protect themselves from predators. The chameleon can change colors to match its surroundings. Some chameleons can change only their color, while others can change both their color and pattern. Lizards that cannot change color have other forms of self-defense. The horned lizard has sharp spikes on its head and back to protect it from its predators. The chuckwalla crawls into a crack in the rocks when it feels threatened, then fills its body with air, making it nearly impossible to get it out of the crack. Finally, some lizards have the ability to shed or break off their tails if a predator grabs on. Later, a new tail will grow in its place. The predator gets the tail but the lizard gets away.

A few lizards eat plants, but the majority of lizards eat insects. This makes them a welcome visitor in many homes, especially in the tropical areas. Komodo dragons, some of the largest living reptiles, eat dead animals. They have a keen sense of smell and will cross large distances to reach a decaying carcass. ■

Animal Camouflage

Draw or paint a picture showing how a chameleon can blend into its surroundings. For example, show a chameleon on a rock. Make the chameleon have a similar color and pattern to the rock, or show it sitting in a tree with similar colors to the leaves. If you have sequins left from the reptile project, you could glue them on the chameleon if they are similar colors to the surroundings. Add this page to your animal notebook.

People Camouflage

Discuss how soldiers use camouflage paint to cover their skin and camouflage clothing to help them blend in with their surroundings. Use face paint to cover your skin to help you blend in with the trees and bushes or other environment you may choose. If you like, someone can take a picture of you in camouflage and you can include it in your animal notebook.

WHAT DID WE LEARN?

- List three ways a lizard might protect itself from a predator.
- What do lizards eat?

TAKING IT FURTHER

- Horny lizards are short compared to many other lizards and are often called horny toads. What distinguishes a lizard from a toad?
- Why might some people like having lizards around?
- How does changing color protect a lizard?
- What other reasons might cause a lizard to change colors?

LARGE LIZARDS

Iguanas are one of the largest lizards in the world. They can grow up to six feet (2 m) long. Although these lizards may look intimidating, they are harmless and only eat plants. Iguanas spend most of their time in trees and are green mottled with brown, which makes them very hard to spot when they are lying in tree branches. God has designed these animals with powerful feet and sharp claws to enable them to easily climb trees. Common iguanas live throughout Central and South America.

Marine iguanas are found only in the Galapagos Islands off the coast of Ecuador. They are the only lizards that spend a significant amount of time in the water. Although the common iguana may leap from a tree into the water to escape an enemy, it primarily lives on land. However, the marine iguanas live along the coast of the islands and spend much of their time in the ocean eating seaweed and algae that grow on the rocks near the shore.

These animals are well suited for swimming in the cold waters around the Galapagos Islands. Since the iguana is a cold-blooded animal it would ordinarily lose much of its body heat as it swims in the cold water. However, the marine iguana's heart rate slows significantly when it dives into the water. This slows down the flow of blood through its body and reduces the amount of heat that it loses. After it is done swimming, the iguana spends much of its time lying in the sun to warm its body back up.

Marine iguana

The marine iguana is designed for swimming. Its wide head and flat tail work to propel it through the water. The marine iguana can stay submerged for up to 20 minutes or more. Although the marine iguana and the common iguana have many different characteristics, they are both the same kind of creature and show that God gave the original iguanas a wide variety of genetic traits.

The largest meat-eating lizard is the Komodo dragon. Do some research and see what you can find out about these interesting creatures. Make a Komodo dragon page for your animal notebook.

Turtles & Crocodiles

Turtle or tortoise, crocodile or alligator—how do you tell?

Lesson 19

What special design features do turtles and crocodilians have?

Challenge words:

carapace

plastron

Beginners

Turtles are the only reptiles that have shells. Some turtles are able to pull their heads and legs inside their shells when they feel threatened. All turtles have scales on their legs, heads, and tails. They lay eggs to reproduce.

Turtles live mostly in warm parts of the world, but a few live where the winters get cold. If a turtle lives in or near the water it is generally called a turtle, but if it lives mostly on the land it is usually called a tortoise. You can look at a turtle's feet to see if it lives in the water or on the land. If it lives in the water it will have flipper-type feet. If it lives on land, it will have claw-type feet.

The largest reptiles alive today are crocodiles and alligators. These animals usually live in the water in warm tropical areas. They can be very dangerous. Crocodiles can stay in the water with just their noses and eyes sticking up above the water. They look like a floating log. They will wait for an animal to come to the edge of the water, and then they attack.

- **What do turtles have that no other reptiles have?**
- **Where do tortoises usually live?**
- **What are the largest reptiles?**
- **How do crocodiles often catch their prey?**

Turtles are the only reptiles with shells. Unlike many sea creatures such as crabs, which can be removed from their shells, turtles' shells are an integrated part of their bodies, not just a home they live in. The shell provides protection for the turtle's internal organs. Also, many turtles can pull their heads, tails, and legs inside their shells when they feel threatened.

Green sea turtle

Giant domed-shaped tortoise

Like all reptiles, turtles have scales covering their skin, are cold-blooded, and lay eggs. Turtles can be found in most warm climates. In some areas with cold winters, turtles will burrow underground and hibernate until warmer weather arrives.

The term *turtle* generally refers to the turtles that live in or near water. Fresh water and sea turtles are equipped with webbed feet or flippers for swimming. Turtles that live mainly on land are generally called tortoises. Tortoises have claws instead of webbed feet, as well as short sturdy legs designed for walking on land. Both turtles and tortoises lay their eggs on land.

Amphibians & Reptiles

Fun Fact

No one knows for sure how long turtles and tortoises live. The Galapagos giant tortoise is believed to live for over 150 years, and many other turtles and tortoises live to be well over 50 years old.

The group of reptiles with the smallest number of species is the crocodiles. This group includes crocodiles and alligators. These can be the largest reptiles alive today with bodies up to 25 feet (7.6 m) long. It is often difficult to distinguish a crocodile from an alligator. Alligators have wider snouts and all of their teeth are covered when their mouths are closed. Crocodiles have longer, narrower snouts and some of their teeth, usually one on the bottom on each side, stick out even when their mouths are closed.

Crocodiles and alligators are generally found in warm tropical climates. They live near water and have webbed

Alligator

Crocodile

Turtle Feet—Tortoise Feet

Purpose: To better understand the difference in turtle and tortoise feet

Materials: tape

Procedure:

1. Tape all the fingers on one of your hands together to represent a turtle's flipper.
2. Make a claw with your other hand.
3. Fill up the kitchen sink with water (or try this in a bathtub or swimming pool) and try pushing the water with your flipper and your claw. Which hand was able to push the most water?

Conclusion: The flipper is much better for swimming. Since a turtle spends most of its time in the water, the flipper is a better design than a claw-like foot. God gave each kind of animal great variability to adapt and survive in its environment.

feet and strong tails that enable them to be good swimmers. Their eyes and nostrils are located on the top of the head and snout, allowing the animal to float with most of its body underwater while it waits for prey to come close enough to attack. A floating crocodile resembles a fallen log floating in the water. When the prey is close, the crocodile snaps its jaws around the victim and drags it underwater, where it holds the prey until it drowns. Crocodiles generally eat turtles, fish, waterfowl, and other small animals. But some larger crocodiles will attack larger animals as well.

Like most reptiles, crocodiles lay their eggs on land. But unlike other reptiles, when the babies are about to hatch, the mother carries the eggs to the edge of the water in her mouth. After they hatch, the mother protects her young for several weeks. Adult crocodiles will eat young crocodiles, so after they leave their mother's protection, they stay away from adults until they are fully grown. ■

Fun Fact

Have you ever heard of crying crocodile tears? Crocodiles often secrete a liquid from their eyes as they are wrestling with their prey. This gives the appearance that they are crying for their victims. Thus, "crocodile tears" refers to insincere sorrow.

What Did We Learn?

- Where do turtles usually live?
- Where do tortoises usually live?
- How does the mother crocodile carry her eggs to the water?
- Why can't you take a turtle out of its shell?
- How do crocodiles stalk their prey?

Taking It Further

- Why might it be difficult to see a crocodile?

How can you tell them apart?

Complete the "How Can You Tell Them Apart?" worksheet by drawing pictures showing how to tell turtles from tortoises and crocodiles from alligators. This worksheet can be included in your animal notebook.

Turtle shells

As you just learned, the turtle is the only reptile with a shell. The shell has a special design which makes it very strong. The top part of the shell covering the turtle's back is called the **carapace** and the bottom of the shell, covering its belly, is called the **plastron**. The carapace and the plastron are connected together at the sides by joints called bridges.

The shell has two layers. The outer layer is made up of epidermal shields that are made of keratin, the same material that fingernails are made of. Below the epidermal shield is a layer of bony plates that are fused to the turtle's ribs and vertebrae.

The sections of the outer layer of the shell are called shields and are arranged in symmetrical shapes. As the turtle grows, new layers of keratin are added under the old layers, making the shell thicker and stronger as the turtle grows. The bony layer of the inner shell is also broken into sections called plates.

When a baby turtle hatches from its egg, it has a fully formed outer shell, but does not have a bony inner shell. As the ribs grow, they send out cells that invade the skin around them turning them into bone. Eventually, the whole area under the epidermal shields is turned into bony plates, creating the strong double-layered shell.

Some turtles can pull their legs, heads, and tails inside their shells. These turtles have hinged plastrons. Once the body is pulled inside the shell, the plastron is pushed up against the carapace, providing protection for the turtle. Turtles that do not have a hinged plastron cannot pull inside their shells.

The leatherback turtle has a unique shell. Instead of the scale-like shields that most turtles have, the leatherback has a rubbery or leathery skin covering its shell. The leatherback is the largest turtle in the world and can be up to 6 feet (1.8 m) long and 8 feet (2.4 m) from tip to tip of its flippers.

In general, tortoises have dome-shaped shells that provide protection from predators while sea turtles usually have flatter, more streamlined shells that are lighter and allow them to glide more easily through the water. God designed the turtle's shell to be strong and effective for its environment.

UNIT 4

ARTHROPODS

KEY CONCEPTS

- **Identify** the characteristics of arthropods.
- **Describe** the five groups of arthropods using examples.
- **Distinguish** between complete and incomplete metamorphosis.
- **Describe** the body plan of insects, arachnids, crustaceans, and myriapods using models.

UNIT LESSONS

Invertebrates

Creatures without a backbone

Lesson 20

Which animals are invertebrates?

Beginners

Most of the animals we have studied so far are ones that you are probably familiar with. But there are many other animals out there that you may not be familiar with. Many of these animals are invertebrates. Invertebrates are animals that do not have backbones. Most of these animals are small.

Invertebrates can be found in every part of the world. Some invertebrates that you might be familiar with include jellyfish, starfish, crabs, shrimp, spiders, ladybugs, and butterflies. You have some invertebrates in your house and in your yard. You may have eaten invertebrates. Many animals eat invertebrates.

We will learn more about the different kinds of invertebrates in the next lessons in this book.

- **What is an invertebrate?**
- **Are invertebrates usually big or small animals?**
- **Where do invertebrates live?**

Although most familiar animals are vertebrates, the vast majority (nearly 97%) of all animals are invertebrates—animals without backbones. Invertebrates do not have internal skeletons; therefore, most of them are small creatures. The squid and the octopus are the only large invertebrates.

The huge variety among invertebrates makes it difficult to group them together. However, scientists have grouped most invertebrates into six groups: arthropods, mollusks, cnidarians, echinoderms, sponges, and worms. In these groups are familiar creatures such as jellyfish, corals, starfish, crabs, shrimp, spiders, ladybugs, and butterflies.

The octopus is a large invertebrate.

INVERTEBRATE REPEAT GAME

This is a simple memory game. Have the first person name an invertebrate. The second person repeats that animal and names a new and different invertebrate. The third person says the first two animals and adds a new one. The game continues until someone breaks the chain or cannot name a new invertebrate.

To help you recognize invertebrates, you can review the vertebrates: mammals, birds, amphibians, reptiles, and fish. Make sure the players understand that they are not to name any of these animals in the game. Think of a few invertebrates to get you started.

This game can be a lot of fun, and will help you realize that invertebrates are really more common than you thought.

Invertebrate Pictionary

Draw a picture of an invertebrate on a white board or piece of paper. While you are drawing have other people guess what the animal is. The first person to guess the correct animal gets to be the next artist.

Invertebrates can be found in every part of the world. Some, such as spiders and insects, may be found in your home. Perhaps you had invertebrates for dinner. You did if you ate shrimp or clams. Earthworms live in your garden. Many more invertebrates live in the waters of rivers, lakes, and oceans.

Many larger animals eat invertebrates for food. The largest creatures of the sea—whales—eat tons of small invertebrates each day. Also, invertebrates help to break down dead organisms to be recycled. We will find God's marvelous creativity all around us as we explore the world of invertebrates. ■

Spiders like this bird-eating spider from Brazil are invertebrates.

What did we learn?

- What are some differences between vertebrates and invertebrates?
- What are the six categories of invertebrates?

Taking it further

- Why might we think that there are more vertebrates than invertebrates in the world?

Invertebrate Collage

Demonstrate your knowledge of invertebrates by making a collage of pictures of various invertebrates to be included in your animal notebook. You can draw the pictures, cut them out of magazines, or print them from your computer. Try to include invertebrates from all six groups mentioned in the lesson. Use an animal encyclopedia or other source for ideas.

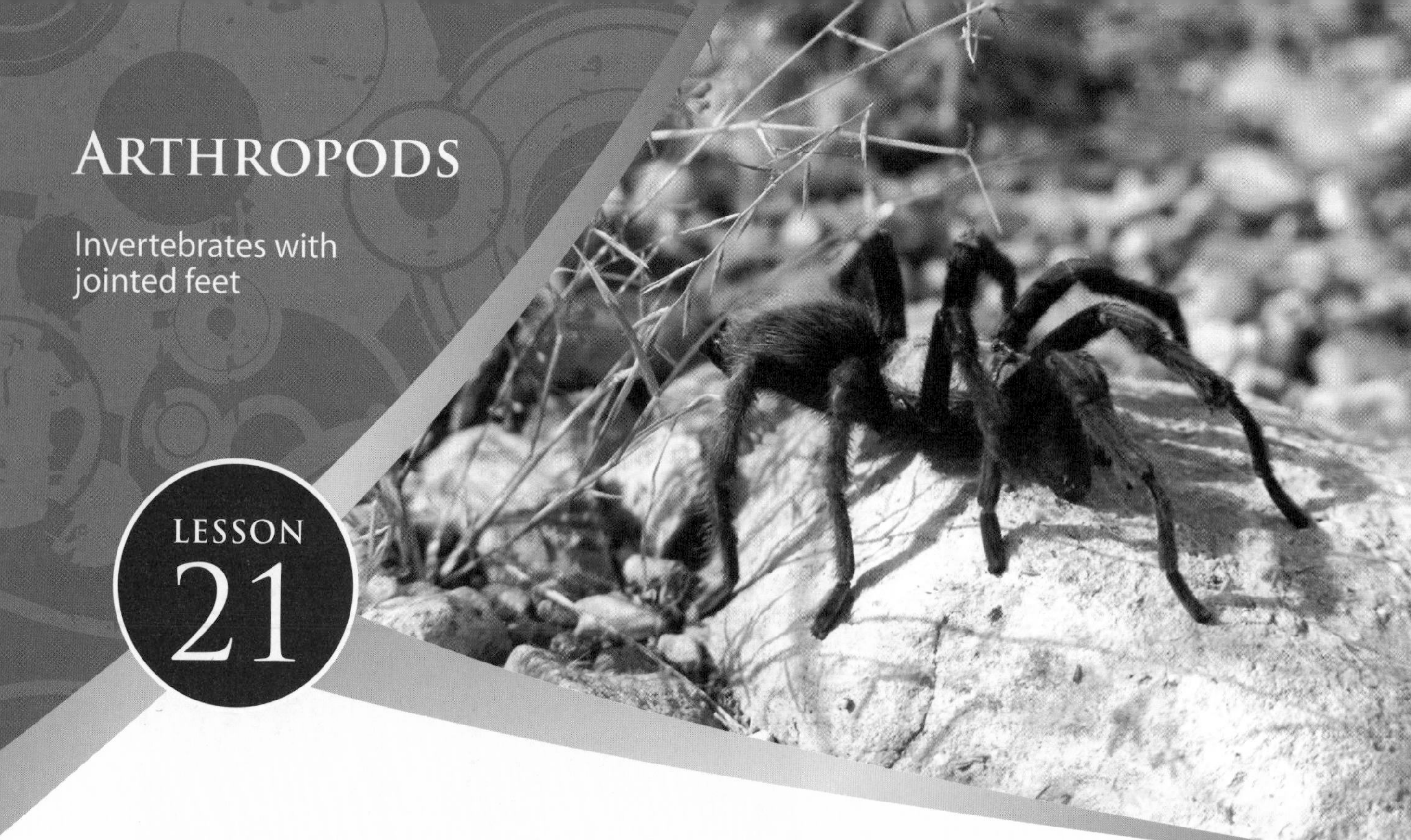

Arthropods

Invertebrates with jointed feet

Lesson 21

What do shrimp, spiders, and mosquitoes have in common?

Words to know:

arthropod

segmented bodies

endoskeleton

exoskeleton

chitin

Beginners

Spiders and insects look a lot alike so you might expect that they could be grouped together. But shrimp, crabs, and millipedes are in the same group as spiders and insects. What do all of these animals have in common? They all have jointed feet or jointed legs. They all have bodies with more than one section. They do not have bones inside their bodies, but have a strong outer coating that is a little bit like armor.

All of these animals are part of a group called **arthropods**. The biggest group of arthropods is the insects. There are over one million different types of insects. How many different kinds of insects can you name? The second biggest group of arthropods is the spiders. We will learn more about these and other groups of arthropods in the next several lessons, and we will see how God specially designed each one.

- **What is the same about the bodies of all arthropods?**
- **What is the biggest group of arthropods?**
- **What is the second biggest group of arthropods?**

The largest group of invertebrates is the arthropods. Over 75% of all animal species are arthropods. **Arthropod** means "jointed foot," so obviously all of the creatures in this group have jointed feet or jointed legs. In addition, all arthropods have **segmented bodies**, meaning they have two or more distinct body regions. Arthropods also have exoskeletons. Instead of an **endoskeleton** which is an internal skeleton of bones or cartilage like vertebrates, arthropods get their protection and structure from an external covering or **exoskeleton**. This outside skeleton is both strong and flexible. It is made of **chitin**, a starchy substance. Exoskeletons do not grow as the animal grows. Instead, the animal periodically sheds its exoskeleton and grows a new one.

Beetles are the largest group of insects, with over 330,000 species.

Of the five groups of arthropods, the largest group is insects (90%). The other groups are arachnids (6%), crustaceans (3%), millipedes (0.8%), and centipedes (0.2%). There are approximately 1 million different species of insects that have been identified, and scientists believe there may be as many as 1 million more species that have not yet been classified. Some of the more common insects include flies, beetles, mosquitoes, butterflies, and ants. Arachnids include spiders, ticks, mites, and scorpions. Nearly all crustaceans live in the sea, and include shrimp, crabs, and lobsters. Centipedes and millipedes are similar creatures, both having multiple body segments and many legs.

As you study this large diverse group of invertebrates, look for evidence of God's design. ■

ARTHROPOD PIE CHART

Use the following information to label the "Arthropod Pie Chart."

- Insects: 1,000,000 species
- Arachnids: 70,000 species
- Crustaceans: 30,000 species
- Millipedes: 10,000 species
- Centipedes: 2,800 species

Include this pie chart in your animal notebook.

Arthropods

WHAT DID WE LEARN?

- What do all arthropods have in common?
- What is the largest group of arthropods?

TAKING IT FURTHER

- How are endoskeletons (internal) and exoskeletons (external) similar?
- How are endoskeletons and exoskeletons different?
- Why should you be cautious when hunting for arthropods?

EXOSKELETON MODEL

One distinctive characteristic of arthropods is their exoskeleton. The exoskeleton is made of a starchy material called chitin.

Purpose: To help you understand how an exoskeleton helps protect an animal's body

Materials: long narrow balloon, string, newspaper, flour, water,

Procedure:

1. Fill a long narrow balloon with air and tie it closed.
2. Tie a piece of string around the middle of the balloon to make two or three body segments. If you do not have a long narrow balloon, you can fill two round balloons with air and tie their necks together to form two body segments.
3. Tear newspaper into strips.
4. Prepare your paste: combine 1 cup of flour with 2 cups of water. Mix to remove all lumps. Add more flour or water as needed to make a smooth paste.
5. Dip one strip of paper at a time in the paste. Slide your fingers along the strip to remove excess paste, then place the strip on your balloon. Be sure to smooth it out so there are no bumps.
6. Add more strips of paper to your model, making sure to overlap the strips. Keep adding strips until the balloon is completely covered.
7. Allow your creation to dry overnight.
8. Repeat the process so that there are two or more layers of paper over the entire model, allowing the strips to completely dry after each layer.

Conclusion: Once you are done, you can feel how the paper with the glue provides a strong covering for the balloons. Flour is made of starch, just like chitin. When it dries it becomes hard just like the chitin. The papier mâché is not as flexible as an arthropod's exoskeleton, but it should help you understand how something like starch can provide protection for insects and other animals.

Insects

Don't let them bug you.

Lesson 22

How can you tell if something is an insect?

Words to know:

- insect
- head
- thorax
- abdomen

Challenge words:

- compound eye
- open circulatory system
- spiracle

Beginners

Do you like insects? It is easy to like ladybugs and butterflies, but not so easy to like mosquitoes. Whether you like them or not, insects are important.

How can you tell if an animal is an insect? You can look closely at its body. An **insect** has three body parts. It has one pair of antennae on its head. An insect has six legs that are all connected to the middle section of its body. And most insects have one or two pairs of wings that are also connected to the middle sections of their bodies.

There are so many different types of insects that we could not mention them all in this book, but we will mention a few that you are probably familiar with. Grasshoppers and crickets are insects with straight wings. Butterflies and moths are insects with large and often colorful wings. Flies, mosquitoes, and beetles are insects as well.

Some insects, such as flies and mosquitoes, may be considered pests. But we need to remember that God created the insects for many purposes. Bees help pollinate flowers and many birds and other animals eat insects for food. So, you see, insects are very important.

- **How many body parts do insects have?**
- **How many legs do insects have?**
- **Name three common insects.**

There are over 1 million species of insects. No wonder you have trouble keeping them out of your house. **Insects** are the largest group of arthropods. In addition to jointed legs and exoskeletons, insects have three distinct body parts. The **head** is the front segment, the **thorax** is the center segment, and the **abdomen** is the back segment. They also have a pair of antennae on their heads, as well as simple and compound eyes. Insects have six legs attached to their thoraxes and most have one or two pairs of wings.

Because there are so many different types of insects, scientists have grouped them into categories by similar characteristics. One group has straight wings. This includes grasshoppers and crickets. Half-wings are the true bugs such as the stinkbug. Butterflies and moths are in their own group. Flies and mosquitoes are in another. Beetles include the stag beetle, weevil, and June bug. There are many other groups of insects as well.

Many insects are pests. They can destroy crops and spread diseases. Insects can cause painful bites, or they can be annoying. However, insects play a very important role in the ecosystem. Birds, reptiles,

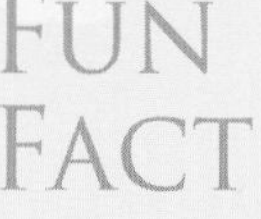

FUN FACT

The bombardier beetle uses its rear-end "cannon" to fire a high-pressure jet of boiling irritating liquid at an attacking predator. The bombardier rapidly mixes two chemicals and injects them into a combustion chamber, which contains mainly water. The beetle then injects a third chemical, which greatly speeds up the normally mild reaction to explosive force. The jet of boiling liquid and gases fires repeatedly (up to 500 pulses per second) through twin "exhaust tubes" at his tail at a stunning 65 feet (20 m) per second.

Insect Models

Purpose: To make an insect model

Materials: three Styrofoam balls, toothpicks, paint, pipe cleaners, paper, scissors

Procedure:

1. Connect 3 Styrofoam balls together with toothpicks to form the body of the insect.
2. If desired, paint the balls the color of the insect; for example, paint it yellow and black if it is a bee or red or black if it is an ant.
3. While the paint is drying, cut pipe cleaners into eight equal-length pieces. You will use six of these pieces as legs.
4. Insert the legs into the center ball (the thorax), three on each side, and bend them to look like legs.
5. Insert the other two pieces of pipe cleaner into the head for antennae.
6. Cut two or four wings from paper. Use brightly-colored paper if you are making a butterfly. Many other insects have translucent wings so you could use white paper or make a frame from pipe cleaners and cover the frame with plastic wrap. If using paper, tape the wing pieces to additional pieces of pipe cleaner and insert them into the center ball.

Conclusion: Discuss each part of the insect as you put it together. Take pictures of the models and include them in your animal notebook.

Water Skipper Model

Purpose: To make a model of a water skipper

Materials: index card, bowl of water

Procedure:

1. Fold an index card in half with long sides together.
2. Trace the pattern below onto the card and cut out the bug shape.
3. Fold the feet out and very carefully place the card in a bowl of water.

Conclusion: The card should float on the surface of the water. Water molecules are attracted to each other and create what is called surface tension. Things that are light enough can stay on the surface of water without sinking. Water skippers and other light insects can walk across the surface of the water without sinking because they are light enough not to break the surface tension.

Water Skipper Pattern

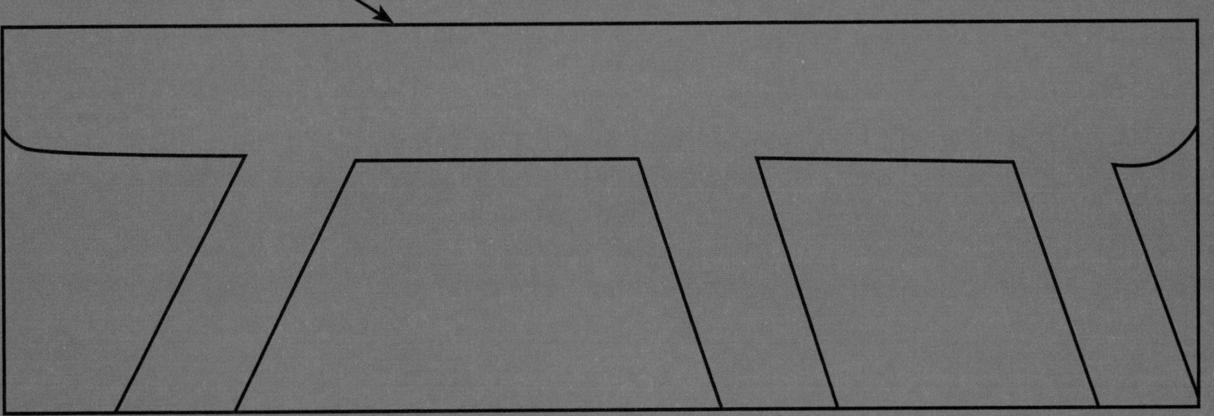

Optional Activity

Playing the game "Cootie" from Milton Bradley is a fun way to review the parts of an insect.

amphibians, and many other animals depend on insects for food. Insects are also very important for pollinating flowers. And some insects, such as butterflies, are very pleasant to have around. As much as we might like to get rid of them, insects are vitally needed. ■

What Did We Learn?

- What characteristics classify an animal as an insect?
- How can insects be harmful to humans?
- How can insects be helpful?

Taking It Further

- How might insects make noise?

Insect Anatomy

The different segments of the insect's body each have special functions. The head serves as the communication center for the animal. The antennae, which are attached to the head, provide a sense of touch, smell, and taste. The antennae on most insects also have tiny hairs that detect sound waves or other vibrations providing a sense of hearing as well.

An insect has two compound eyes, one on each side of its head. **Compound eyes** have multiple lenses fitted together like a mosaic. Each lens can see only a small area, but the images from all the lenses are combined together to give the insect a good view of what is around it. In addition to compound eyes, many insects also have simple eyes, which can detect light and shadow and some movement.

Different insects have different abilities to see. Flies and mosquitoes are very near-sighted and can only see a few millimeters away from their heads, but can see a very wide area around them. Butterflies are very sensitive to color and find their food by the color of the plants. Other insects are completely color-blind. Dragonflies have very acute eyes and can detect and identify other flying objects while flying themselves.

The thorax is the center for movement. The legs and wings are both attached to this segment so walking and flying are both coordinated here. The thorax is divided into three sections and one set of legs is attached to each section. The wings are attached to the middle section as well.

The abdomen contains most of the insect's internal organs. Insects have most of the same internal systems that vertebrates have. Even though an insect's internal organs may seem simple compared to the systems of vertebrates, they are still incredibly complex. The insect digestive system is similar to a bird's digestive system in many ways. It contains a crop for holding food and a gizzard for grinding the food up before it enters the stomach. Nutrients are absorbed primarily through the stomach since insects do not have small intestines.

Insects have a very different circulatory system from most vertebrates. Insects do not have closed blood vessels to carry the blood throughout the body. Instead, the heart pumps blood into the head. The blood then flows toward the rear of the insect through its body chamber around all of the internal organs. This is called an **open circulatory system**. The heart is a tube-like organ that runs the length of the abdomen. It has many tiny valves all along its surface that allow blood to flow from the body into the heart to be pumped again toward the head.

Finally, insects do not have lungs or gills like vertebrates. Instead an insect has openings call **spiracles** in the sides of it body. Air flows through the spiracles into air sacs that run throughout the insect's body. Exchange of oxygen and carbon dioxide occurs in these air sacs. The insect's abdomen expands and contracts to force the air to move throughout its body.

If you look closely, you can see the compound eyes of this killer bee.

Arthropods

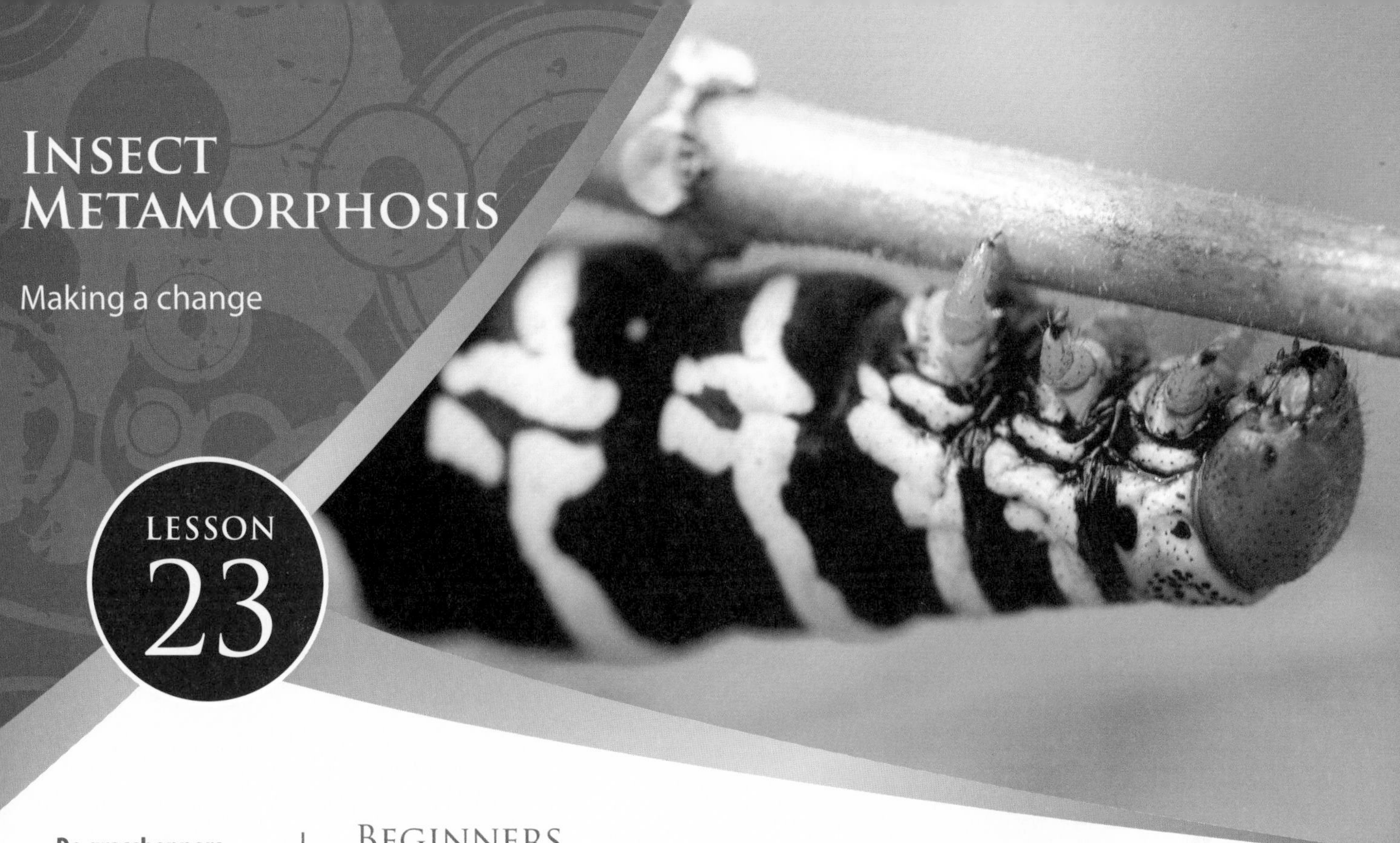

Insect Metamorphosis

Making a change

LESSON 23

Do grasshoppers and butterflies undergo the same type of metamorphosis?

Words to know:

incomplete metamorphosis

complete metamorphosis

nymph

larva

chrysalis

pupa

Challenge words:

bioluminescence

Beginners

What do baby insects look like? First a mother insect lays an egg. Some insects, like grasshoppers, hatch from their eggs and look very much like their parents only smaller. As the grasshoppers grow, they develop wings and soon become adults. The baby insect that looks like its parent is called a **nymph**. There are three stages to a grasshopper's life: egg, nymph, and adult.

However, most insects do not look like their parents when they hatch from their eggs. Most baby insects look very different from their parents and must go through a big change to become an adult. The baby insect that does not look like its parent when it hatches is called a **larva**. You are probably familiar with a caterpillar. A caterpillar is a butterfly larva, but it looks much more like a worm than a butterfly. After hatching, an insect larva eats and grows until it is time for it to change into an adult.

When it is ready to change into an adult, a larva forms a chrysalis around itself. A **chrysalis** is a protective shell. While it is in the chrysalis, the insect's body changes completely. It no longer looks like a worm, but develops the three body parts, along with six legs and wings of an adult insect. When the change is complete the insect comes out of its shell and begins life as an adult. Most insects have four stages in life: egg, larva, chrysalis, and adult. We don't know why God designed insects to experience such a big change in their bodies, but it is amazing to watch it happen.

- **What are the three stages of a grasshopper's life?**
- **What are the four stages of a butterfly's life?**

All insects reproduce by laying eggs. However, what hatches out of the egg may or may not look anything like the parents. Most insects go through a metamorphosis, or change, between birth and adulthood.

Some insects, such as grasshoppers, go through **incomplete metamorphosis**. This means the young resemble their parents when they hatch and gradually change into an adult. There are three stages to an insect's life if it experiences incomplete metamorphosis: egg, nymph, and adult. The **nymph** hatches from the egg, and then as it grows it molts or sheds its exoskeleton several times. As it gets bigger, the nymph begins growing wing pads. After its final molt, the insect has complete wings and is considered an adult. Dragonflies, crickets, termites, and grasshoppers are some of the insects that experience incomplete metamorphosis.

The six stages of grasshopper development from newly hatched nymph to adult

Most insects experience a 4-stage life cycle called **complete metamorphosis**. An insect that goes through complete metamorphosis starts out as an egg. When it hatches, it is called a **larva** (plural: larvae). The larva of the butterfly is a caterpillar. Other insect larvae also resemble caterpillars. The larva does not look much like the adult that it will become.

FUN FACT

The firefly is the state insect for both Pennsylvania and Tennessee.

As the larva grows, it spends most of its time eating. Its exoskeleton cannot grow

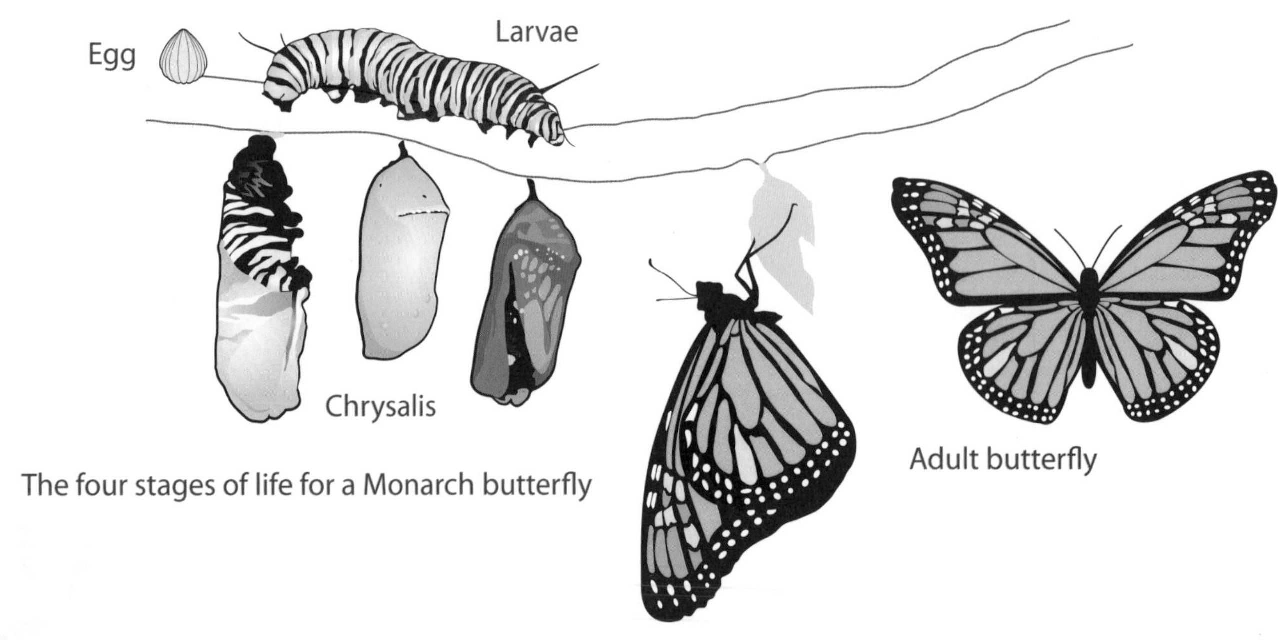

The four stages of life for a Monarch butterfly

Arthropods

FUN FACT

Monarch butterflies are one of the few insects that migrate with the changing seasons. Huge groups of monarchs can sometimes pass through an area for several days or even weeks as they migrate between the U.S. and Mexico. Monarchs have been known to migrate more than 1,500 miles.

with it, so it sheds the exoskeleton several times as it grows. After a few days or weeks, the larva enters the third stage of its life, called the **chrysalis** or **pupa** stage. During this stage, the larva's body undergoes a tremendous change. This stage can last from a few days to a few months, depending on the type of insect.

When the change is complete, the insect breaks out of its chrysalis and is an adult. The most dramatic change to witness is the changing of a caterpillar into a butterfly, but other insects experience drastic changes as well. Witnessing this change is an amazing experience. ■

METAMORPHOSIS WORKSHEET

Draw and color the different stages of metamorphosis on the "Stages of Metamorphosis" worksheet. Include this worksheet in your animal notebook.

BUTTERFLY BREAKOUT

Place two scarves inside a sleeping bag. Pretend to be a caterpillar and crawl into the sleeping bag. You should remain very still while in the sleeping bag, just as the pupa does not move inside the chrysalis. Then, unzip the sleeping bag and emerge holding the scarves and using them like wings. You have become a butterfly.

OBSERVE METAMORPHOSIS

The very best way to appreciate the changes that occur in complete metamorphosis is to actually observe them. Many science supply catalogs sell live caterpillars that can be kept and observed while they turn into butterflies (or you might be able to find a caterpillar in the fall, and keep it in a jar until it forms a chrysalis). The butterflies can then be released if the weather is favorable.

WHAT DID WE LEARN?

- What are the three stages of incomplete metamorphosis?
- What are the four stages of complete metamorphosis?

TAKING IT FURTHER

- What must an adult insect look for when trying to find a place to lay her eggs?

FIREFLIES

One insect that has an unusual characteristic throughout all stages of metamorphosis is the firefly (or lightning bug). Even though its name might imply that it is a fly, the firefly is really a beetle. This beetle has the ability to glow. It can glow inside its egg, it can glow as a larva, and it can glow as an adult.

The process by which a firefly glows is called **bioluminescence**. This is a chemical reaction that takes place inside the insect's body that produces a pale green light. A protein in the insect's abdomen reacts with a chemical called luciferase when air enters the chamber containing the two substances. This chemical reaction gives off light. The firefly can control the flow of air and thus controls the light that is given off.

The light that is produced by bioluminescence is a cool light because the process is very efficient. Nearly 96% of the energy is turned into light, so very little heat is produced. In an incandescent light bulb the majority of the energy is turned into heat. This is why light bulbs get quite hot. But fireflies and other light-producing animals have the ability to produce light with very little heat.

Scientists are unsure why firefly eggs emit light. It is believed that larva emit light as a warning to predators since many species of firefly larva contain substances that are poisonous to predators. As adults the main purpose of emitting light is to attract a mate. Each species sends out a different series of flashes to identify itself. The male firefly emits light while flying and the female firefly answers with her own light from her location on the ground or in a tree. Thus the light guides the male to the female. In areas where there are many species of fireflies, each species emits light at a different time, similar to different frog species croaking at different times. This synchronized lighting allows more individual species to communicate with each other.

Arthropods

Arachnids

Spiders and such

LESSON 24

How do spiders keep from getting caught in their own webs?

Words to know:

arachnid

cephalothorax

spinnerets

Challenge words:

urticating hairs

Beginners

Many people think that insects and spiders are the same type of animal. But there are some important differences. An insect has three body parts but a spider has only two body parts. An insect has six legs, but a spider has eight legs. Also, spiders do not have any wings or antennae.

Almost all spiders can spin webs. They have special parts on the back of their bodies, which produce silky string. The spider takes these long thin threads and weaves them into a web. Most of the threads in the spider's web are sticky, and the spider uses the web to catch insects for dinner. A few of the threads are not sticky and the spider uses those threads to move around without getting caught in the web.

Other animals that are classified with spiders include scorpions, mites, and ticks. Mites and ticks look very much like spiders so you may not be surprised that they are grouped together, but scorpions look rather different. However, scorpions have eight legs just like spiders. They also have two body parts. They look different because their back body section is jointed and curls up, but scientists put them in the same group as spiders.

- **How many legs does a spider have?**
- **How many body parts does a spider have?**
- **What do insects have as part of their bodies that spiders do not have?**
- **Why does a spider spin a web?**

Many people wonder if spiders are insects. Despite some similarities in their looks, there are several differences between insects and spiders. Insects have three body parts, whereas spiders have only two body parts. Also, insects have six legs and spiders have eight. These differences place spiders in the class of arachnids.

Arachnids have two body parts. The front segment is called the **cephalothorax** and is essentially a head and thorax fused together. The rear segment is called the abdomen. Arachnids also have eight legs which are attached to the cephalothorax. Arachnids lack wings and antennae which is another difference between them and insects.

Fun Fact

Dragline silk, the main support for a spider's web, is a hundred times stronger than steel. It has been calculated that a cable made from this silk a little thicker than a garden hose could support the weight of two full Boeing 737 airplanes. The silk used in web spirals can stretch more than 200%.

Spider and Scorpion Models

Purpose: To make a spider and scorpion model

Materials: marshmallows, toothpicks, pipe cleaners, marker

Spider model—Procedure:

1. Connect two large marshmallows with a toothpick. These are the two body parts.
2. Cut two pipe cleaners into four pieces each and insert them into the front marshmallow (four on each side).
3. Bend the pipe cleaners to resemble legs.
4. You can draw eyes on the front of the spider with a marker if you want to. Note the different parts as you assemble the model.

Scorpion model—Procedure:

1. You will use one large marshmallow for the cephalothorax.
2. Using a piece of flexible wire or pipe cleaner, string several small marshmallows together for the abdomen and attach them to the end of the large marshmallow.
3. Bend the wire up so the small marshmallows resemble a tail with a stinger.
4. Use pipe cleaners to make eight legs and stick them into the large marshmallow.
5. Twist a small piece of pipe cleaner onto the end of each of the front legs to make claws. Remember that scorpions are venomous.

Take pictures of the models to add to your animal notebook.

Optional—Spider Snacks

For a fun snack, you can make edible spider snacks. Use a round cracker for the cephalothorax. Spread peanut butter on the cracker. Add raisins for eyes. Add eight pretzel sticks to the cephalothorax for legs. Add another round cracker to one edge for the abdomen. Spread peanut butter on this cracker as well. Yum!

Optional—Looking at a Web

If you have the opportunity, closely observe a real spider's web. Use a magnifying glass to look at the individual strands. Sprinkle a light powder, such as powdered sugar, on the web. It will stick to the sticky strands but not to the non-sticky ones.

FUN FACT

Ballooning helps some spiders to avoid over-crowding and competition for food. Spiderlings climb to the highest point they can find. They tilt their abdomen and spinnerets upward as they release silk. The strand of silk lengthens and is picked up by the breeze and the spiderlings are pulled upward and travel to a new location.

Spiders are the most common arachnids. They can be found throughout the world. Most spiders spin webs and kill their prey with venom. But only a few spiders are poisonous to humans. Spiders do not have mouth parts for biting or chewing. They can only suck liquids from their prey. Spiders have special organs at the back of their abdomen called **spinnerets** that produce the silk thread used in weaving webs. If you closely examine a spider's web, you will find that some of the strands are smooth and some are sticky. The spider can move easily around its web by walking on the smooth strands. Also, spiders secrete an oily substance on their feet that keeps them from sticking to their own webs.

Spiders are not the only creatures in the arachnid family. Mites, ticks, and scorpions are also arachnids. Mites and ticks resemble small spiders. However, they do not spin webs or catch insects. Instead, like many other parasites, they attach themselves to other animals and suck their blood. For many creatures, mites and ticks are a nuisance. But for some, including humans, mites and ticks can carry and spread serious diseases. That is why it is always a good idea to check for ticks after hiking in the woods or other areas where ticks live.

At first glance, scorpions may not seem to fit in with spiders, ticks, and mites. But a closer examination shows that, like spiders, scorpions have eight legs attached to a cephalothorax, as well as an abdomen. The scorpion's abdomen is jointed and curls behind it, ending in a stinger. Scorpions can inflict a painful sting and should be avoided. ■

A scorpion

WHAT DID WE LEARN?

- How do arachnids differ from insects?
- Why are ticks and mites called parasites?

TAKING IT FURTHER

- Why don't spiders get caught in their own webs?

Arthropods

Tarantulas

Tarantulas do not spin webs as most other spiders do. Instead, the tarantula will hide near its burrow waiting for an unsuspecting animal to walk near. Most spiders have poor eyesight and the tarantula is no exception. The tarantula senses its prey through vibrations and through feeling with its legs and feet. When an animal walks within range, it attacks with its fangs and injects venom into its victim. Once the animal is dead, the spider injects it with digestive juices, which liquefy the body and allow the spider to suck up its dinner. Although the largest tarantulas have been known to eat birds, lizards, mice, and other animals, most small tarantulas eat large insects such as crickets, grasshoppers, and beetles.

Tarantulas can be found in nearly every part of the world. The largest ones are found in South America. Most tarantulas are gray or brown, but some species have brightly-colored spots on their legs or abdomens. Their bodies are covered with fine hair. They are generally inactive during the day and hunt at night.

Although tarantulas are deadly to their prey, they are not considered to be dangerous to humans. Although people have been accidentally bitten by tarantulas, this usually results only in a swollen spot that is itchy but quickly heals. Tarantulas also protect themselves with special barbed hairs, called **urticating hairs**, that they can rub off their abdomen and kick toward an enemy. These hairs can cause itching and irritation in skin or eyes and encourages enemies to back off. Despite the very slight chance of being bitten, many people keep tarantulas as pets.

It takes several years for a tarantula to completely mature. Once a male matures, he searches for a female to mate with. After mating, the male quickly leaves because female tarantulas are known to eat males. Males usually live only a few months after mating. Females, on the other hand, can live for 10 to 20 years after becoming mature.

Arthropods

Fun Fact

Tarantulas are the largest spiders known to man. There are over 800 species of tarantulas with leg spans ranging from 2 to 11 inches (5–28 cm). In many other countries tarantulas are called bird spiders, reflecting the fact that the largest spiders can catch and eat birds and other animals.

Crustaceans

Are they crusty?

Lesson 25

Where do we find crustaceans?

Words to know:

crustacean

Beginners

The word crustacean may be new to you, but I bet you know about some of the animals that are crustaceans. Have you ever seen a crab or lobster? Have you ever dug up a pill bug or roly-poly? If so, then you have seen a crustacean. **Crustaceans** are similar to insects and spiders because they have jointed legs and two distinct body parts. Most crustaceans have tough outer shells.

One crustacean that may live in a stream near your house is a crayfish or crawdad. These interesting animals have ten legs. The front legs end in pincers that help them catch their food and defend themselves from enemies. God put its mouth on the underside of its body, so a crayfish eats food from the bottom of the riverbed. Crayfish look very much like small lobsters. Other crustaceans live in the ocean. These include shrimp, crabs, and tiny animals called brine shrimp and water fleas. Even these tiny animals are important because they provide food for other animals.

- **Name three crustaceans.**
- **How many body parts does a crustacean have?**
- **Why is the crayfish's mouth on the underneath side of its body?**

Have you ever chased a crawdad in a stream, or eaten shrimp or lobster? Have you ever watched a crab burrow in the sand or dug up a roly-poly? If so, then you are familiar with crustaceans. Most crustaceans live in the water with the notable exception of the woodlouse (sometimes called a pill bug or roly-poly).

All **crustaceans** are arthropods with jointed legs and exoskeletons. In addition, crustaceans have two distinct body parts or regions: the cephalothorax and the abdomen. They also have two pairs of antennae, two or more pairs of legs, and gills for breathing in the water.

The crawdad, or crayfish, is a very familiar crustacean found in many fresh water streams. Crayfish have two pairs of antennae on their heads that help them sense

White speckled lobster

Crayfish

Clay models

Make clay models of several different crustaceans. Note the similarities and differences between the animals. Take pictures of the models to add to your animal notebook.

Woodlouse exploration

If weather permits, search for a woodlouse. Because they breathe with gills, they must stay in moist areas, so they can usually be found under rocks or pieces of wood, or in other protected areas. If you find one, examine it carefully with a magnifying glass. Pay close attention to its jointed legs, antennae, exoskeleton, and segmented body.

food or enemies. They also have five pairs of legs attached to the cephalothorax. The front legs end in pincers, or claws, which they use for catching prey or defending themselves. God put its mouth on the underside of its body, so a crayfish eats food from the bottom of the riverbed. Also, a crayfish can evade an enemy by darting backward very quickly.

You may be most familiar with the larger crustaceans such as crabs, shrimp, lobsters, and crayfish. But the majority of crustaceans are very small—mostly microscopic. Many sea creatures today depend on these tiny animals, such as brine shrimp and water fleas, for food. Many whales have special "teeth," called baleen, which they use to strain these tiny crustaceans from the water. ■

Many crustaceans, such as shrimp, are eaten for food.

WHAT DID WE LEARN?

- What do all crustaceans have in common?
- What are some ways that the crayfish is specially designed for its environment?

TAKING IT FURTHER

- Why might darting backward be a good defense for the crayfish?
- At first glance, scorpions and crayfish (or crawdads) look a lot alike. How does a scorpion differ from a crayfish?
- How can something as large as a blue whale survive by eating only tiny crustaceans?
- If you want to observe crustaceans, what equipment might you need?

CRUSTACEAN RESEARCH

There are many interesting crustaceans that you may not be familiar with. Do some research in an animal encyclopedia, on the Internet, or other source and find out what you can about the animals listed below. Create one or more pages in your animal notebook using the information you find on the following animals:

- Krill
- Plankton
- Cleaner shrimp
- Barnacles
- Water slater

Myriapods

How many shoes would a centipede have to buy?

LESSON 26

How do you tell the difference between a millipede and a centipede?

Words to know:

myriapod

centipede

millipede

Beginners

The word **myriapod** comes from the word for many feet. The animals that are myriapods definitely have many feet. Centipedes and millipedes are the animals that are myriapods.

Centipedes (pictured above) have flattened bodies with about twenty segments. Each segment has a pair of legs so centipedes have about 40 legs all together. The first set of legs on a centipede has venomous claws so be sure not to touch a centipede or it may bite you.

Millipedes, on the other hand, are not venomous. They are very round and have two pairs of legs on each body segment. A millipede can have as many as 100 segments so it can have as many as 400 legs. Millipedes and centipedes both like to live in dark moist places, so be careful when you dig in the dirt or move big rocks.

- **What does myriapod mean?**
- **Which myriapod has venomous claws?**
- **How can you tell a centipede from a millipede?**

Centipedes and millipedes are called **myriapods**. The word *myriapod* means "many feet." Centipede means "100 feet" and millipede means "1,000 feet." But, do centipedes and millipedes really have that many feet? Not necessarily, but they do have a lot of feet. Let's see just how many feet they have.

Centipedes usually have between 15 and 25 body segments. Each segment has one pair of legs, so a centipede has between 30 and 50 legs. Its first pair of legs has venomous claws that are used to kill its prey. Centipedes also have long antennae and a flattened body that is usually a few inches long.

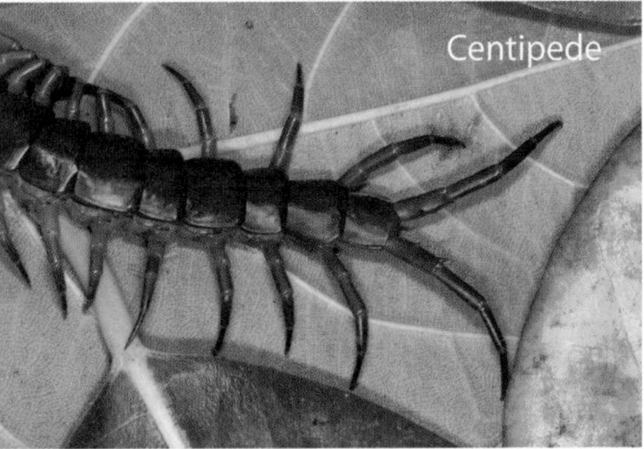
Centipede

Millipedes differ from centipedes in several ways. First, they have rounded bodies, not flat bodies. Also, they are not venomous. But the most distinctive difference is that they have two pairs of legs per body segment instead of only one pair. Millipedes usually have between 44 and 400 feet, but not 1,000. Millipedes tend to be bigger and slower than centipedes and have shorter antennae. Both centipedes and millipedes live in dark moist places.

Centipedes and millipedes are sometimes confused with caterpillars. However, caterpillars do not have legs on every body segment.

Millipede

Fun Fact

The millipede with the most legs ever was first discovered in California in 1926. *Illacme plenipes* was first spied by a government scientist in San Benito County, about 120 miles southeast of San Francisco. He counted a record-making 750 legs.

Arthropod Baseball

Set up a "baseball diamond" by assigning places such as chairs or pieces of paper on the floor to be home, first, second, and third base. Set a chair in the middle as the pitcher's mound. An adult gets to be the pitcher and each student gets to be a batter. The batter selects the difficulty of the pitch: single, double, triple, or home run. The pitcher selects an appropriate question about arthropods. For example, "Name the 5 groups of arthropods." The batter must answer the question. If the answer is correct, the batter advances to the appropriate base (e.g., 1 base for a single, 2 bases for a double; the harder the question, the more bases the question is worth). Then the next batter gets to answer a question.

If the batter cannot correctly answer a question, it is considered an out. After three outs, the adult gets to be the batter and the students get to ask the questions. See who can score the most runs.

Also, caterpillars experience metamorphosis and change into butterflies or moths. Centipedes and millipedes do not change into another form. Caterpillars are often fuzzy and live in the open on different plants, while myriapods are usually smooth and live in dark places such as under rocks or under the ground. ■

WHAT DID WE LEARN?

- How can you tell a centipede from a millipede?
- What are the five groups of arthropods?
- What do all arthropods have in common?

TAKING IT FURTHER

- What are some common places you might find arthropods?
- Arthropods are supposed to live outside, but sometimes they get into our homes. What arthropods have you seen in your home?

MYRIAPOD MODELS

Purpose: To demonstrate your understanding of the differences between centipedes and millipedes by making models of each

Materials: modeling clay, pipe cleaners or craft wire, camera

Procedure:

1. Use modeling clay to make each segment.
2. Flatten the body of the centipede and make sure the millipede is round.
3. Use pipe cleaners or craft wire to add legs to each segment. Be sure to add one set of legs to each segment of the centipede and two sets of legs to each segment of the millipede.
4. Take a picture of each of your models to include in your animal notebook. Feel free to add drawings or photographs, too.
5. Add any interesting information you can find on these myriapods.

UNIT 5

Other Invertebrates

KEY CONCEPTS

- ◊ **Describe** the three groups of mollusks using examples.
- ◊ **Illustrate** the two-part life cycle of cnidarians.
- ◊ **Describe** the basic characteristics of echinoderms.
- ◊ **Describe** two ways that sponges reproduce.
- ◊ **Identify** three kinds of worms.

UNIT LESSONS

MOLLUSKS

Creatures with shells

LESSON 27

Do all mollusks have shells?

Words to know:

mollusk

mantle

bivalve

gastropod

cephalopod

Challenge words:

buoyant

BEGINNERS

Have you ever walked along the seashore and found a seashell? That shell was once the home of an animal that is called a **mollusk**. You are probably familiar with some of the mollusks. Some of these animals have two parts to their shells. These include oysters and clams. They can open and close their shells. Sometimes you might find a pearl inside of an oyster.

Other mollusks have one-piece shells. A snail is an example of this kind of mollusk. Each type of mollusk produces a different kind of shell so you can tell what kind of animal lived in the shell just by its shape and color.

A few mollusks do not have shells. These include the octopus and the squid. Squids and octopuses move through the water by squirting a jet of water out the back. They can also spray a jet of black ink into the water to confuse their enemies. The octopus is considered one of the most intelligent animals without a backbone.

- **What kinds of mollusks have two-piece shells?**
- **Name a kind of mollusk that has a one-piece shell.**
- **How does a squid move through the water?**
- **Which is considered the most intelligent mollusk?**

As you walk along the beach you are likely to find a variety of sea shells. Most of these shells are the remains of mollusks. **Mollusks** are soft-bodied invertebrates. They have non-segmented bodies with no bones. A mollusk has one muscular foot for moving about, a hump containing the internal organs, and a **mantle**, which is an organ that secretes a substance that hardens into a shell in most species. Most, but not all, mollusks live in the water.

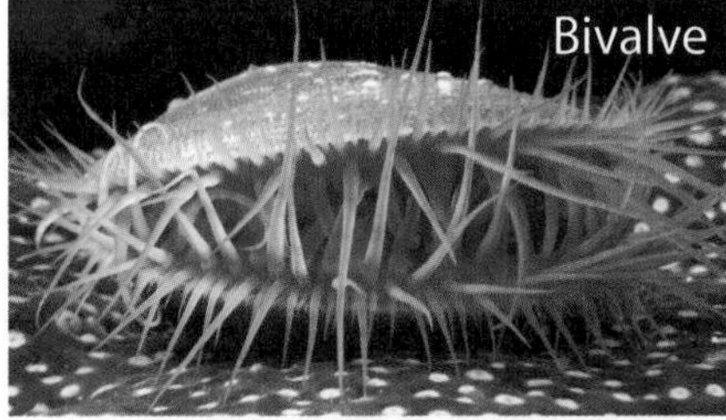
Bivalve

Although all mollusks have these characteristics, there is great variety among them. Mollusks that have two-part shells are called **bivalves**. Oysters, clams, scallops, and mussels are all bivalves. The shells of these mollusks are connected by a hinge at the back and are opened and closed by strong muscles. Many bivalves produce a pearly substance that protects the internal organs from irritants that get inside their shells. Oysters produce a shiny substance that, after a period of years, turns the irritants into pearls that are prized by people.

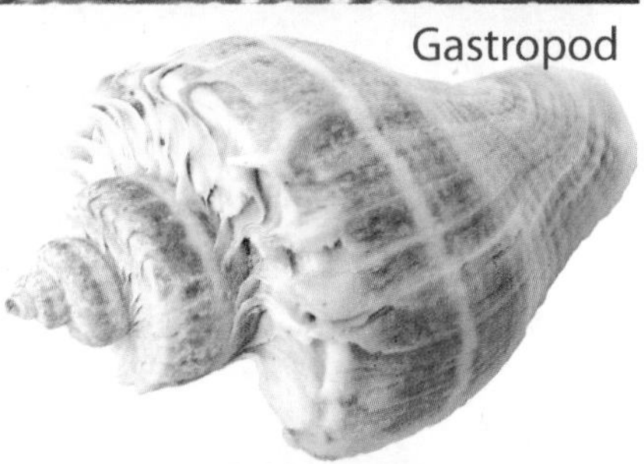
Gastropod

Many mollusks have only one-piece shells. These are called **gastropods**. Gastropods include snails, conchs, abalones, and slugs. With the exception of slugs, gastropods produce beautifully-spiraled shells. Each species produces a unique style of shell, so shells can be used to identify the animal.

Slug

The third group of mollusks is the **cephalopods**. This group includes squids, octopuses, and nautiluses. At first glance, this group may not seem to fit the characteristics of mollusks. However, a closer examination reveals a foot merged with the head, a hump containing the internal organs, and a mantle. In some cephalopods, the mantle produces an outer body wall and not a rigid shell.

Squids and octopuses can move quickly through the water by jet propulsion. Also, both creatures can spray out an inky substance to confuse their enemies and get away when they feel threatened. Both squids and octopuses have complex eyes that are similar in design to the eyes of vertebrates. Evolutionists have a very hard time explaining how creatures with such supposedly different evolutionary chains as octopuses and humans, ended up with such similar and complex eyes. We know, however, that God designed them both.

Cephalopod

SHELL IDENTIFICATION

Collect as many different shells as you can. Each mollusk generates a unique shape of shell; therefore, you can tell what animal used to live in it if you have a guide to help you. Use a shell guidebook to help you identify what creature used to live in each of your shells. Which shells were bivalves (two parts)? Which shells were gastropods (one part—spiraled)?

Take pictures of your shells and include the pictures and identifications in your animal notebook.

The giant squid that lives in the Pacific and North Atlantic Oceans can grow to be 60 feet (18 m) long, weigh up to 1 ton, and is the largest invertebrate. Although they are large, they are often food for an even larger vertebrate—the sperm whale. Octopuses, though not as large as the giant squid, have a complex brain and are considered to be one of the most intelligent invertebrates. ■

WHAT DID WE LEARN?

- What are three groups of mollusks?
- What body structures do all mollusks have?
- How can you use a shell to help identify an animal?

TAKING IT FURTHER

- How are pearls formed?

THE NAUTILUS

A very interesting cephalopod is the nautilus. Like the octopus and squid, the nautilus has many tentacles. It uses these tentacles to grasp its food. The nautilus eats lobsters, shrimp, and crabs. After grasping the food, it then breaks open its food with its sharp beak. Also like the octopus, the nautilus is nocturnal. It hides during the day, usually in deep water, and hunts in shallower water at night.

Unlike the octopus and squid, the nautilus has a permanent shell. This shell has many chambers inside. It is believed that the first four chambers of the shell form while the nautilus is still inside the egg. As the nautilus grows, the shell grows and adds more chambers. The animal itself actually lives in the largest chamber of the shell. As new chambers are added to the shell, water is pumped out of the innermost chambers and gas takes its place. This allows the animal to remain **buoyant**, able to float, in the water even as its shell gets bigger and heavier. If the animal feels threatened, it can pull its body inside its shell and close a leathery flap over the opening.

Cephalopods move by sucking in water, then pushing the water out the back of their bodies in a powerful stream that shoots the animal forward. In the nautilus, the funnel which takes in the water contains gills, allowing the nautilus to breathe as water flows through its body.

Purpose: To demonstrate the type of propulsion used by cephalopods

Materials: water balloon, bathtub

Procedure:

1. Fill a bathtub with several inches of water.
2. Fill a small balloon with water but do not tie it closed.
3. Place the balloon in the tub and let go of the neck of the balloon.

Conclusion: The water will shoot out the neck of the balloon, forcing it to race through the water. Of course the balloon does not have any control over the flow of the water so it may move recklessly about the tub, but cephalopods can control the flow and are very agile in the water.

Cnidarians

Jellyfish, coral, and sea anemones

LESSON 28

Why are cnidarians so dangerous to most animals?

Words to know:

coral

coral colony

coral reef

cnidarian

polyp

planula

medusa

symbiotic relationship

Challenge words:

siphonophore

Beginners

A jellyfish is a very interesting creature, but it is not a fish. It has a bell-shaped body that looks like it is made of jelly and it has lots of long tentacles. Jellyfish capture their food by stinging fish or other sea creatures with the poison in their tentacles. Most animals avoid jellyfish, but there are a few fish, like the clownfish, that are protected from the jellyfish's sting.

An animal that is similar to a jellyfish is a coral. It may not seem like coral are similar to jellyfish at all. But that is because you are probably familiar with the shells that coral build around themselves and not with the animal itself. A **coral** is a tiny creature with long tentacles. It builds a case around itself for protection. Thousands of tiny coral live closely together and their shells combine to form the beautiful **coral colonies** and **reefs** that you may be familiar with. But if you look at the tiny animals that live inside the crusty shells, you will see that they look like tiny cousins to the jellyfish.

The sea anemone is also similar to coral and jellyfish. An anemone has a hollow body with long stinging tentacles just like the coral and jellyfish. It is much larger than a coral but can be smaller than a jellyfish. All of these creatures are beautiful and designed by God to live in the ocean.

- **Why do most fish try to stay away from jellyfish?**
- **How does a coral protect itself?**
- **What animal is similar to coral and jellyfish?**

What do jellyfish, coral, and sea anemones have in common? They all have hollow bodies and stinging tentacles, so they are grouped together as cnidarians. **Cnidarian** (ni-DARE-ee-un) means "stinging tentacles." Cnidarians spend at least part of their lives in the form of polyps. A **polyp** has a cylinder-shaped body with tentacles and a mouth on top.

Polyp stage of a cnidarian

This description of a polyp may not make you think of a jellyfish, but the jellyfish goes through many changes in its life cycle (see illustration below). It begins life as an egg. The egg hatches into a **planula**, which looks like a worm. The planula settles on the sea bottom and grows into a polyp. It may remain in the polyp stage for up to a year. Eventually, disks grow at the top of the polyp. When these disks break off they become medusas. When the **medusas** are mature, they have the jelly-filled bodies we consider to be adult jellyfish. Jellyfish inhabit nearly all parts of the ocean. Jellyfish have stinging

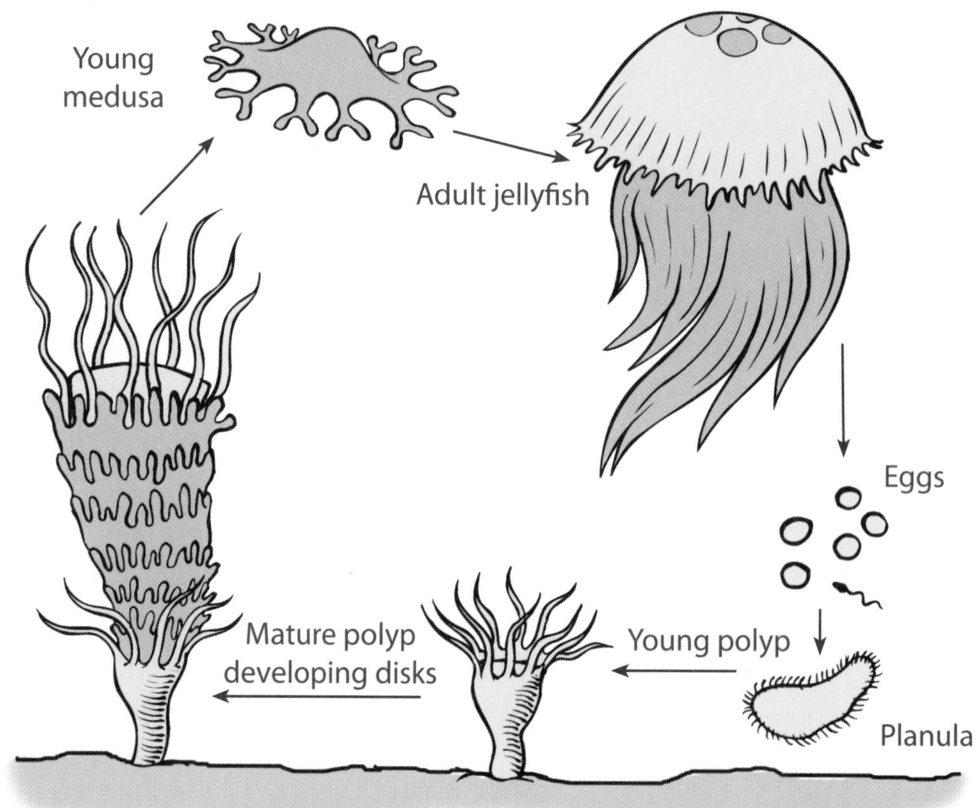

Other Invertebrates

Coral Reef

Make a model of a coral reef. Look at pictures of different kinds of coral. Then use clay, marshmallows, pretzel sticks, or any other craft supplies you have available. Glue these items together on a cardboard base to make a model of a coral reef. Take a picture of your reef and include it in your animal notebook.

tentacles, so most creatures stay away from them. A few animals, such as the clownfish, have special protection from the stings and can live closely with jellyfish.

Coral may not appear to be similar to jellyfish but their design is very similar to the polyp stage of the jellyfish. A coral also begins life as an egg that hatches into a larva. The larva settles on the sea bottom and begins secreting a calcium-based substance. This substance hardens into a case around the larva. The larva then develops into a polyp. Hundreds of thousands of polyps live together to form a **coral colony**. Millions of coral colonies create a **coral reef**. Coral polyps stay inside their hard cases when threatened, but when hunting, the polyps come out and shoot poison arrows at their prey. Then the polyps' tentacles pull the stunned food into their hollow bodies.

Plume worm

Sea anemone

Sea anemones have a similar polyp body structure to jellyfish and coral. They are often brightly colored and catch their prey with their long stinging tentacles.

Several cnidarians have **symbiotic relationships** with other creatures, relationships where both benefit. For example, some corals have an algae living inside them. This algae produces food for the coral, while the coral provides protection for the algae. Also, some fish that are not harmed by jellyfish live near them. When a larger fish attacks the smaller fish, the jellyfish stings the attacker, then both the jellyfish and the smaller fish share the meal. ■

Fun Fact

Lion's Mane jellyfish are the world's largest jellyfish. In the Arctic, specimens can reach 8 feet (2.4 m) in diameter and their tentacles can reach up to 100 feet (30 m) long.

WHAT DID WE LEARN?

- What characteristics do all cnidarians share?
- What are the three most common cnidarians?

TAKING IT FURTHER

- How do you think some creatures are able to live closely with jellyfish?
- Why do you think an adult jellyfish is called a medusa?
- Jellyfish and coral sometimes have symbiotic relationships with other creatures. What other symbiotic relationships can you name?

MAN O' WAR

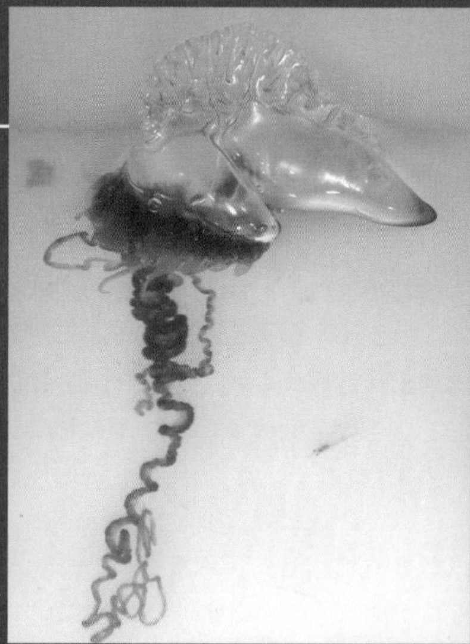

The Portuguese Man O' War is a cnidarian that is often called a jellyfish; however, it is actually a siphonophore (sī-FON-u-for), not a jellyfish. A **siphonophore** is a collection or colony of cnidarians living together in a symbiotic relationship.

Each creature forming the Man O' War has a special purpose. One creature forms the float, which is an air-filled pouch that keeps the colony floating on the surface of the ocean. Other creatures form tentacles, which sting fish and other sea creatures for food. Some creatures in the colony provide digestion and others are in charge of reproduction. This is truly a group effort.

The Man O' War can have very long tentacles that dangle in the water. These tentacles can be up to 60 feet (18 m) long. These tentacles have a very powerful sting and have been know to kill people. They do not attack people, but swimmers have become tangled in the tentacles and have died from the stings.

The float on a Man O' War has a flat band across the top, which works like a sail to catch the wind and move the creature through the water. Another siphonophore that also sails through the water is called the by-the-wind sailor. A by-the-wind sailor has shorter tentacles than the Portuguese Man O' War and has a flatter float with a broader sail shape on top. These sailors often float together in large groups up to 60 miles (100 km) across. Sometimes the wind blows them to shore and thousands can be seen trapped on the beach.

Although you don't want to touch cnidarians because of their stinging tentacles, you can observe some pretty harmless creatures in this group. Hydras are tiny, often microscopic, cnidarians that live in fresh water. They have the familiar hollow body shape with multiple tentacles for catching food. You can order samples of live hydras from a science supply store and view them with a magnifying glass or microscope. They can be fascinating to watch. For a fun research project, find out how hydras reproduce.

Echinoderms

Spiny-skinned creatures

LESSON 29

How many legs does a starfish have?

Words to know:

echinoderm

regenerate

Challenge words:

water vascular system

circular canal

sieve plate

ray canals

tube feet

Beginners

How many legs does a starfish have? If you have ever seen a starfish you know that most of them have five legs around the center of their bodies. The starfish (also called a sea star) has a mouth on the bottom of its body in the very center. It is covered with spiky skin and is usually found on the floor of the ocean.

Starfish eat clams and oysters. A starfish will use its legs to pry open a clam shell. It only needs to open the shell a little bit. Then it sticks its stomach out through its mouth and into the shell. It can then digest the clam while it is still in its shell.

Starfish have another amazing ability. They can grow back a leg if it is cut off. In fact, even if the starfish is cut in half, it can grow an entire new half of its body. Look at pictures of different starfish in an animal encyclopedia to see how many different starfish there are.

- **How many legs does a starfish have?**
- **What is a starfish's skin like?**
- **What amazing abilities does the starfish have?**

Echinoderms (ee-KINE-o-derms) are spiny-skinned animals. These creatures have hard spikes made from calcium carbonate. **Echinoderms** also have a system of water-filled tubes that help them move. The most familiar echinoderms are starfish, sea urchins, and sand dollars. Most echinoderms have a central disk with five rays going out from the disk. This design is easily seen in starfish but can be observed in sand dollars as well.

Sea urchin

Starfish (or sea stars) are the most well known echinoderms. These spiky creatures have five (sometimes more) arms coming from a central disk. They are flexible and can move quickly along the sea floor. Starfish mainly eat clams and oysters. A starfish can grip a clam or oyster and pull on its shell until the creature tires. If the clam opens its shell only a fraction of an inch, the starfish will turn its own stomach inside out through its mouth. Forcing its stomach into the crack, the starfish then digests the clam while it is still in its shell. When it is done eating, the starfish pulls its stomach back inside its body and moves on.

Sand dollar skeleton

Starfish also have the ability to **regenerate** or grow back a missing body part. If one of its limbs is cut off, it can grow another one.

Sea urchins, sand dollars, and starfish all begin as eggs, hatch into larvae, and then grow into adults. Sea urchins have very long spikes. Sand dollars have very short spikes. Echinoderms are often very brightly colored. ■

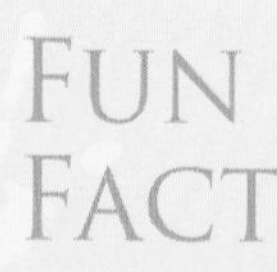

Fun Fact

The largest starfish ever collected came from the southern Gulf of Mexico in 1968. It measured over 51 inches (1.3 m) from tip to tip of its long, thin arms, but its body disc was only about 1 inch (2.6 cm) in diameter.

Starfish Model

Use salt dough to form a 5-legged starfish on a piece of tag board or cardboard. Try to make the model thicker in the middle and thinner at the ends of the legs. Gently press mini-chocolate chips into the starfish to represent spikes. Take a picture of this model to include in your animal notebook.

Observing Echinoderms

If possible, obtain a real (dead) starfish or sand dollar. These are sometimes available at craft or novelty shops. Observe each creature with a magnifying glass. Look for five legs and spiny skin. A sand dollar does not have five legs, but does have markings for five sections.

WHAT DID WE LEARN?

- What are three common echinoderms?
- What do echinoderms have in common?

TAKING IT FURTHER

- Why would oyster and clam fishermen not want starfish in their oyster and clam beds?
- What would happen if the fishermen caught and cut up the starfish and then threw them back?
- What purpose might the spikes serve on echinoderms?

WATER VASCULAR SYSTEM

As you just learned, echinoderms move via a **water vascular system**, which is a series of tubes that are filled with water. Let's take a look at exactly how this works in a starfish. The starfish has a central disk that contains its internal organs. Around the circumference of this disk is a tube called the **circular canal**. This tube is connected to the outside of the starfish through the **sieve plate** which is a series of holes that allows water to flow into the circular canal.

Water is pumped from the circular canal into each of the legs or rays of the starfish through a series of tubes called **ray canals**. The ray canals run the length of each ray and split off into two rows of tubes which go to the tube feet. **Tube feet** are rows of tubes that line the bottom of each ray.

When water is pumped into the tube feet, they expand. Then when the water is released into the ocean, this creates a vacuum causing the feet to become suction cups. This expanding and contracting movement allows the starfish to move quickly along the bottom of the ocean floor and to be able to grip its prey.

You can better understand the anatomy of a starfish if you actually dissect one or observe a dissection. You can order dissecting materials from a science supply store and follow the instructions that come with the specimen. Or if you prefer just to watch a dissection, you can find several sites on the Internet that show step-by-step photos of an actual starfish dissection.

Draw a diagram of the starfish water vascular system. Label all of the parts. Include this diagram in your animal notebook.

Other Invertebrates

Sponges

How much water can a sponge hold?

LESSON 30

Is a sponge really an animal?

Words to know:

sponge

pores

Challenge words:

biomimetics

fiber optics

Beginners

Have you ever used a sponge to wash dishes or to help wash your mom's car? What did it look like? It probably had lots of holes in it. A sponge is good for washing things because it can absorb a lot of water through the holes. Most sponges are made from a type of soft plastic, but you might not know that some sponges come from animals that used to be alive.

Like a kitchen sponge, an animal **sponge** is full of holes, too. It lives on the bottom of the ocean and water flows through all the holes in its body. The sponge traps its food as the water flows through its body. A sponge looks more like a plant than an animal, but it produces eggs, which turn into new sponges, so it is an animal.

Sponges have something in common with starfish. If you cut a sponge in half, it will grow into two new sponges. But sponges do not have legs or mouths like starfish.

- **What does a sponge have all through its body?**
- **What happens to a sponge when you cut it in half?**

One of the simplest multi-celled invertebrates is the **sponge**. Sponges attach themselves to the sea floor. They have tube-like bodies with no complex systems. It is believed that sponges do not even have nerve cells. What sponges do have is lots of holes.

Water flows into **pores**, which are small openings or holes in the sides of the sponge. Oxygen and microscopic organisms are removed from the water as it flows through the sponge. Then the water and any waste products are released through an opening on the top of the sponge.

Like starfish, sponges can regenerate. If even a small piece is cut off of a sponge, it can grow into a new sponge. In fact, some sponge farmers grow sponges by cutting them up, attaching them to cement blocks, and lowering the blocks into the sea.

Sponges are often found in the same areas as coral. When an area becomes too crowded, a sponge may become aggressive and overgrow a colony of coral. Sponges are immune to the poison darts shot out by coral and can eventually overtake a coral colony.

For many years, sea sponges were harvested for use as cleaning tools. However, synthetic sponges are now much more popular and real sponges are used less frequently.

Scientists originally thought sponges were plants because they do not move. But studies have shown that sponges do not produce their own food so they cannot be plants. Also, sponges can reproduce with eggs and the larvae do move around before anchoring themselves to the sea floor, thus classifying them as animals. ■

WHAT DID WE LEARN?

- How does a sponge eat?
- How does a sponge reproduce?
- Why is a sponge an animal and not a plant?

TAKING IT FURTHER

- Why can a sponge kill a coral colony?
- What uses are there for sponges?
- Why are synthetic sponges more popular than real sponges?

SPONGE PAINTING

Have your teacher help you cut synthetic sponges (the kind you get at the grocery store) into the shapes of jellyfish, coral, starfish, sand dollars, and other sea creatures. Create an underwater picture by dipping each sponge into paint and pressing it on a piece of paper. When it is dry, this picture can be added to your animal notebook.

If a real sea sponge is available, examine it closely. Compare and contrast a real sea sponge with a synthetic sponge. How are they alike? How are they different? Which one would you prefer for cleaning your house?

Biomimetics

Sponges are one of the simplest animals that exist, yet they amaze scientists with their design. Scientists at Lucent Technologies' Bell Labs are involved in the study of **biomimetics**, which is the study of living creatures to find ways to apply their designs to human technology.

One amazing discovery that these scientists have made is the discovery of fiber optic materials in sponges. **Fiber optic** applications use very thin glass strands to carry signals of light for telephone transmissions and other communications. The sponges being studied are called Venus Flower Basket sponges. These sponges have a crown of fibers at their bases made from silica, the same material that glass is made from. Although they are not clear enough for communication purposes, these strands can transmit light. What makes them so amazing, however, is that these fibers are much stronger than man-made fibers and resist breaking and cracking. Scientists are continuing to study these fibers to see how they can make man-made fibers stronger.

Another biomimetic project at Bell Labs is studying the eyes of the brittle star, a type of starfish. The lenses on these starfish are very tiny crystals imbedded in their skin, which work together to form a compound eye. These microlenses are very good at reducing distortion. Scientists are developing similar crystals to use in electronic optical systems to achieve much clearer images.

A third project is studying a protein from jellyfish that glows. Doctors are experimenting with injecting this protein into cancer patients. The glowing protein points out cancerous tissue allowing the doctor to be more precise in his surgeries.

So what can we learn from biomimetics? First, we can see that even the "simplest" creatures are extremely complex. They have more to teach us than many people in the past have thought. Second, we see that God's design is better than man's design. Man can always learn from what God has created. Third, we see that God's creation declares His glory. So even though you are studying "simple" animals, remember that they are not really simple at all.

Worms

Creepy crawlers

LESSON 31

Why are some worms important and others dangerous to humans?

Words to know:

flatworm

roundworm

segmented worm

compost

Challenge words:

hydrothermal vent

tube worm

chemosynthesis

plume

hemoglobin

Beginners

Have you ever gone fishing and used worms as fish bait? Many people think that worms are only good for catching fish. But earthworms are good for something else, too. Earthworms are small animals that live in the ground. They are long and thin and round. They do an important job. They eat dead plants and turn them into fertilizer. This fertilizer helps new plants to grow. So earthworms are important because they help plants to grow better.

Earthworms are the kind of worms you are most likely to see. Most soil has earthworms living in it. However, there are other kinds of worms that you might not see very often. Some worms are flat instead of round. **Flatworms** often live in water. Other worms are round and smooth and are called **roundworms**. Earthworms have bodies with lots of rings around them, and are called **segmented worms**, but roundworms do not have any rings. Roundworms are usually harmful to people and animals so it is better to stay away from them. Earthworms are harmless to people and can help plants, so they are good to have around.

- **What do earthworms look like?**
- **What do earthworms eat?**
- **Why are earthworms helpful?**
- **Name two kinds of worms other than earthworms.**

If you are a fisherman, then you probably know where to find worms. To many people earthworms are nothing more than fish bait. However, worms are much more important than that. There are three main groups of worms: segmented worms, flatworms, and roundworms. All are long and narrow and have very simple bodies.

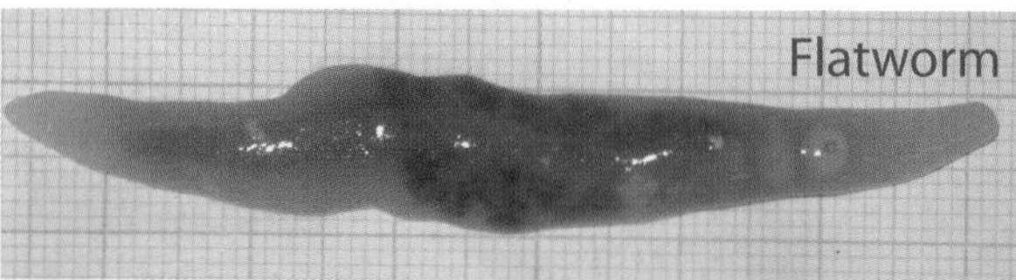

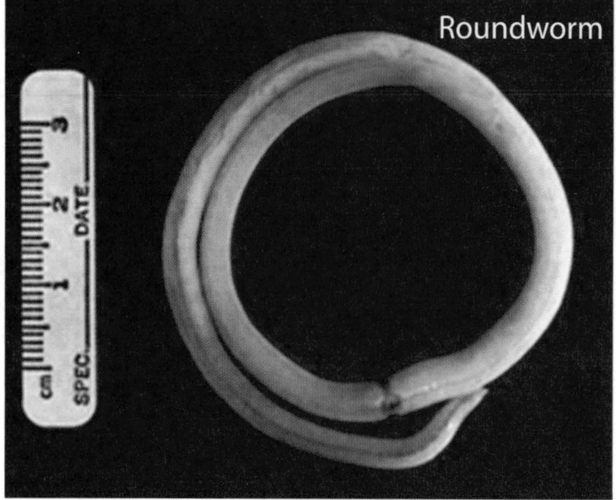

Segmented worms, worms with rings, are the most common. Nearly everyone is familiar with the earthworm. This creature loves moist earth. It eats dead plant material, turning it into fertilizer, or **compost**, for plants to use. This is why worms are so important. Segmented worms are great composters. Many people raise worms to use in compost bins. You feed your food scraps to the worms and they turn it into compost or fertilizer for your garden. Sea worms, leeches, and ragworms are also segmented worms.

The second type of worm is the **flatworm**. As the name suggests, these are flat creatures. Most flatworms live in water or are parasites living inside animal hosts. Planarians are flatworms that live in water. They have arrow-shaped heads and are usually less than one inch (2.5 cm) long. Planarians have a great ability to regenerate and, if cut into pieces, all but the tail will grow into a new worm. Flukes and tapeworms are both parasitic flatworms. They survive by infesting a host animal and absorbing nutrients from it. Parasitic worms are very dangerous, and often deadly, to their hosts.

The third group of worms is **roundworms**. These long, thin, smooth worms are almost all parasites. They often live in the intestines of a host and suck the host's blood or absorb digested food. They are almost always harmful to the host. So, depending on the type of worm, it can be very harmful or very beneficial to humans. ■

Worm Diorama

Make a scene in a shoebox showing an earthworm's habitat. Include dirt, rocks, dried leaves, and any other items you might find where earthworms live. Use gummy worms for the earthworms. Take a picture of your diorama for your animal notebook.

Wormy Snack

Mix instant chocolate pudding according to package directions. Place about an inch of crushed chocolate cookie crumbs in the bottoms of four plastic cups. Put a gummy worm in each cup with one end hanging over the rim. Divide the pudding between the cups. Add another layer of cookie crumbs. Now you have four yummy mud pies with worms for dessert!

WHAT DID WE LEARN?

- What kinds of worms are beneficial to man?
- How are they beneficial?
- What kinds of worms are harmful?

TAKING IT FURTHER

- How can you avoid parasitic worms?

TUBE WORMS

Until the 1970s, it was believed that all ecosystems depended on sunlight and plants to perform photosynthesis for food; from all observations, every animal in an ecosystem either eats plants or eats other animals that eat plants. However, in the 1970s a very unusual ecosystem was discovered that changed this belief. On the bottom of the ocean floor, scientists discovered **hydrothermal vents**, areas where super-heated water flows from under the ocean floor. This water contains large amounts of hydrogen sulfide and other minerals.

Living around these hydrothermal vents are very special kinds of worms called giant tube worms, which can grow up to 8 feet (2.4 m) long. These **tube worms** do not eat plants or animals, yet they are thriving. So how do they get their food? Living inside the tube worms are millions of tiny bacteria. The tube worms absorb oxygen, hydrogen sulfide, and carbon dioxide from the water. The bacteria convert these compounds into carbohydrates which provide energy for the tube worms. This process of converting chemicals into energy is call **chemosynthesis**.

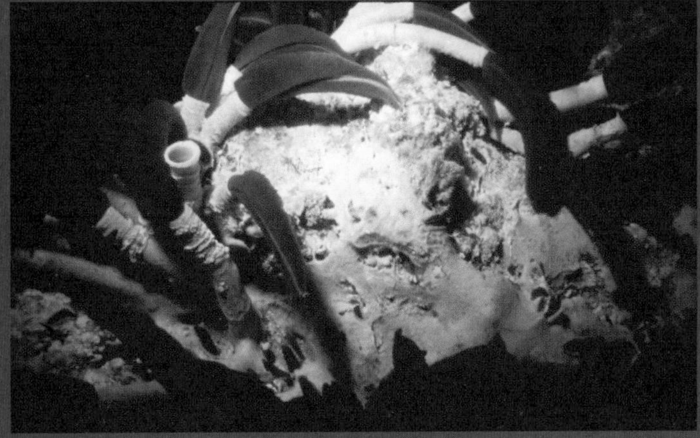

Just as coral and algae have a symbiotic relationship, the tube worms and the bacteria also have a symbiotic relationship. The tube worms provide protection and shelter for the bacteria, and the bacteria convert chemicals into food for the worms.

Tube worms live inside tubes made of chitin, the same material that forms the exoskeletons of insects and crustaceans. These tough tubes protect the worms' soft bodies from potential predators. The bodies of the tube worms are soft and round like other worms. The end of a tube worm's body is called its **plume**. The plume on many tube worms is bright red, due to the hemoglobin that flows through the plume. **Hemoglobin** is a substance that turns bright red in the presence of oxygen. Some tube worms are missing their plumes because crabs or other animals living nearby are sometimes fast enough to get in a bite before the worm is able to pull into its tube.

It is a testimony to God's incredible design that anything can live in the deep dark waters near hydrothermal vents. The surrounding water is extremely cold, the water coming from the vents is extremely hot, there is no sunlight, and the pressure is unimaginable. Yet, there is a thriving ecosystem containing at least 500 different organisms that survive due to God's great design. Draw or paint a picture of this amazing ecosystem to include in your animal notebook.

UNIT 6

Simple Organisms

KEY CONCEPTS

◊ **Describe** the differences between monerans and protists.

◊ **Identify** the relationship between human health and protists, monerans, and viruses.

UNIT LESSONS

Kingdom Protista

Simple creatures?

Lesson 32

Are protists simple?

Words to know:

- protist
- cell membrane
- nucleus
- cytoplasm
- mitochondria
- vacuole
- flagellate
- flagellum
- sarcodine
- pseudopod
- ciliate
- cilia
- gullet

Challenge words:

- sporozoan
- plasmodium

Beginners

You have learned about many different kinds of animals. Some of them were probably old friends and others were new to you. Today you are going to learn about creatures that are so tiny you can only see them with a good microscope. These creatures are called **protists**. Many of them are so small that they only have one cell. Even those that are only a single cell can still do many of the same things that bigger animals do such as eat, move, and reproduce.

One type of protist is a euglena. This tiny creature has a special tail that spins like a motor to propel it through the water. A second kind of protist is an amoeba. Amoebas can move by changing their shape. An amoeba pushes its cell out in one direction like a finger, then moves the rest of the cell into that area. So amoebas have constantly changing shapes. A third type of protist is the paramecium. A paramecium is shaped like a submarine and is covered with tiny hairs. These hairs wave back and forth to move the cell through the water. And finally, algae are protists. They may look like plants, but they are not.

Protists are found nearly everywhere there is water. Protists live in lakes, ponds, rivers, and streams. The water you drink probably does not have many protists because it has been purified, but water in nature is the perfect home for these little creatures.

- **What are single-celled creatures called?**
- **How does a euglena move?**
- **How does an amoeba move?**
- **How does a paramecium move?**

Some of the simplest life forms are **protists**. However, these microscopic creatures are more complex than you might think. Protists have all of the basic parts of an animal cell including cell membrane, nucleus, cytoplasm, mitochondria, and vacuoles. The **cell membrane** acts like skin—providing protection. The **nucleus** acts like the brain and controls the cell's functions. The **cytoplasm** provides a transportation network for the various parts of the cell. The **mitochondria** are the cell's power plants; they break down food and provide energy. And the **vacuoles** are the cell's warehouses, providing food storage.

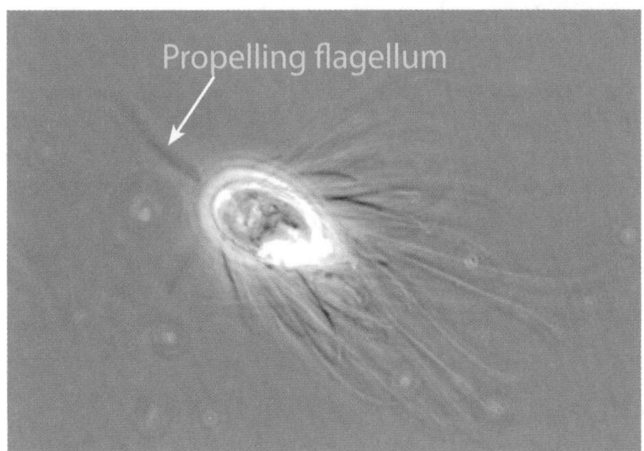

The flagellate above is propelled by the single flagellum on the left. The other flagella are not used for movement.

In addition, most protists have specialized parts that allow them to perform many of the functions that larger creatures do. They eat and digest food, move, and protect themselves. There are thousands of protists. Scientists have grouped them by the way they move.

Flagellates are single-celled creatures that move by using a **flagellum**, or whip-like structure, at the front of the cell. A euglena is a common flagellate found in freshwater lakes and ponds. It uses its flagellum like an outboard motor to propel itself through the water.

The euglena is a puzzling creature because, even though it has the characteristics of an animal

Paramecium Model

Make a model of a paramecium. For the body outline, trace your shoe on a piece of construction paper and then cut it out. Glue short pieces of yarn around the edges to represent the cilia. You can cut different colors of paper to represent the nucleus, vacuoles, and mitochondria and glue them to the model. Note: this is a two dimensional or flat model. Actual paramecium are more submarine shaped and covered all over with cilia. Add this model to your animal notebook.

Observe Microscopic Creatures

If you have a microscope available, examine a drop of pond or stream water. Look for tiny creatures that live in the water. You may be able to observe some of the creatures discussed in this lesson as well as slightly larger creatures.

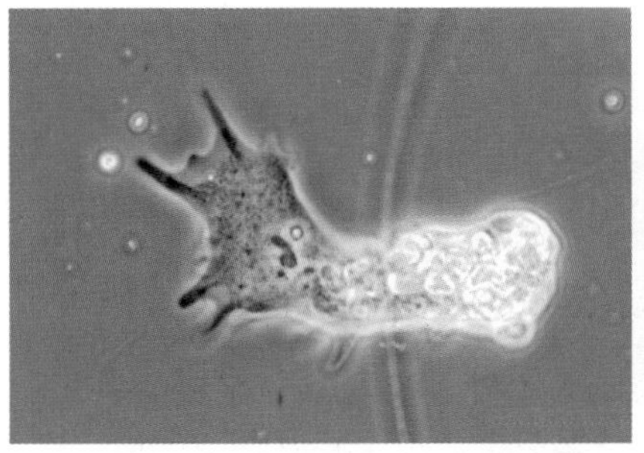
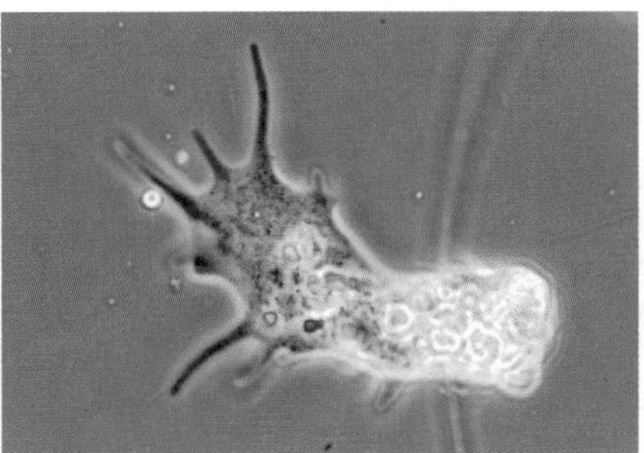
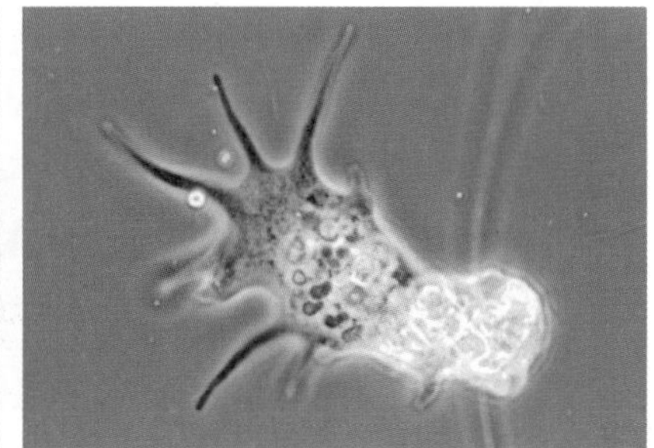

The amoeba above is propelled forward by several pseudopods.

and has the ability to catch food, it also has chlorophyll in its body and can produce its own food. Because of this and other anomalies, protists are put into a kingdom of their own (Protista) and are not part of the animal kingdom.

The second type of protist is the **sarcodine**. These are single-celled creatures with a pseudopod. **Pseudopod** means "false foot." A sarcodine moves by extending one part of its cell membrane in a finger- or foot-like projection and then moving the rest of the cell into that area. The amoeba is the most familiar creature with pseudopods. It is continually moving by changing its shape. An amoeba generally has several pseudopods sticking out at any one time. An amoeba ingests food by extending two or more pseudopods to surround the food and then take it into its cell.

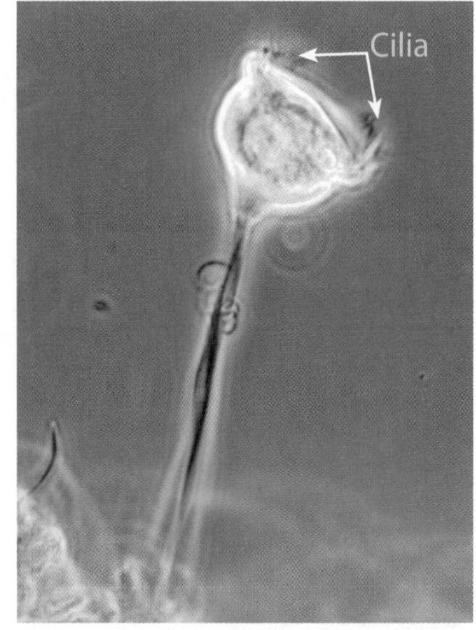

The ciliate above uses its cilia to capture food while anchoring itself on a stalk.

The third type of protist is the **ciliate**. Ciliates are single-celled animals that are surrounded by **cilia**, or hair-like projections, that propel them through the water. A paramecium is a common ciliate. A paramecium is a submarine-shaped cell. The actual paramecium is covered all over with cilia. Its cilia not only move it around, but also push food into its **gullet**, an opening that serves as its mouth.

Algae are plant-like organisms that are classified as protists. There are both single-celled algae and multi-cellular algae. Microscopic forms that live suspended in the water column of the ocean (called phytoplankton) provide food for many small marine animals.

Most protists live in water. Many are parasitic and cause some very serious diseases such as malaria, African sleeping sickness, and amoebic dysentery. Protists generally reproduce by some sort of division where one cell divides to form two new cells. Even though some people consider these to be simple life forms, they are actually very complex, and God's amazing design is obvious in their complex functions. ■

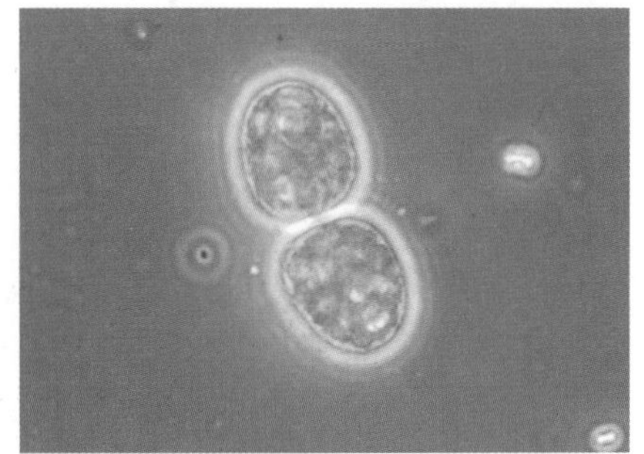

A protist completes a reproductive division

WHAT DID WE LEARN?

- How are protists different from animals?
- How are they the same?

TAKING IT FURTHER

- Why is a euglena a puzzle to scientists?
- Why are protists not as simple as you might expect?

SPOROZOANS

One group of protists, called sporozoans, are very dangerous to people and animals. **Sporozoans** are single-celled creatures that produce spores that infect animals and humans with dangerous diseases. These protists generally have very complicated life cycles. They reproduce asexually, by dividing, and later on they reproduce sexually with sperm and eggs.

One of the most well known sporozoan is the **plasmodium**, which causes malaria. The plasmodium is injected into a human host when an infected mosquito bites a human. The spores of the plasmodium enter the blood stream where they are carried to the liver of the victim. Inside the liver, the spores begin reproducing. Eventually the new spores break out of the liver and enter the blood stream. Here the spores infect red blood cells.

Inside the red blood cells the sporozoans again reproduce asexually until the cell bursts open. This releases new sporozoans into the blood stream where they again infect more red blood cells. It also releases toxins into the blood.

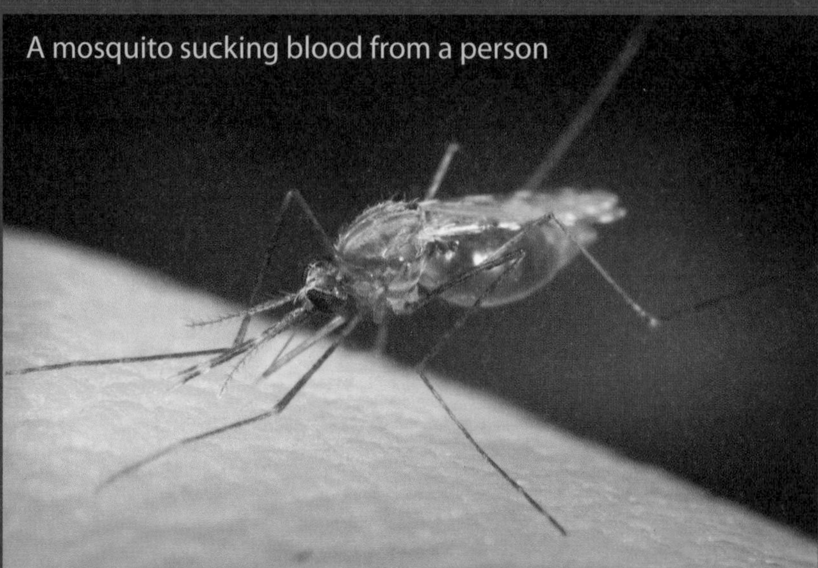
A mosquito sucking blood from a person

These toxins are what cause the symptoms of malaria including chills, fever, thirst, and fatigue.

Eventually, inside the red blood cells, female and male cells are produced. When these cells enter the blood stream they do not infect other cells. However, when a mosquito bites an infected person, some of these male and female cells are ingested by the mosquito. Inside the mosquito's digestive system, these cells combine to form new sporozoans. The new cells travel to the mosquito's salivary glands where they are then transmitted to a new victim.

This complicated life cycle has made it difficult for doctors to treat malaria. Many anti-malaria drugs kill the sporozoan cells in the blood stream, which relieves the malaria symptoms. However, the sporozoans in the liver can stay hidden for months and may cause a new outbreak of symptoms after the patient thinks he is cured. Some drugs treat both the spores in the blood and in the liver. Malaria infects approximately 500 million people each year and nearly 2.7 million people die annually from the disease.

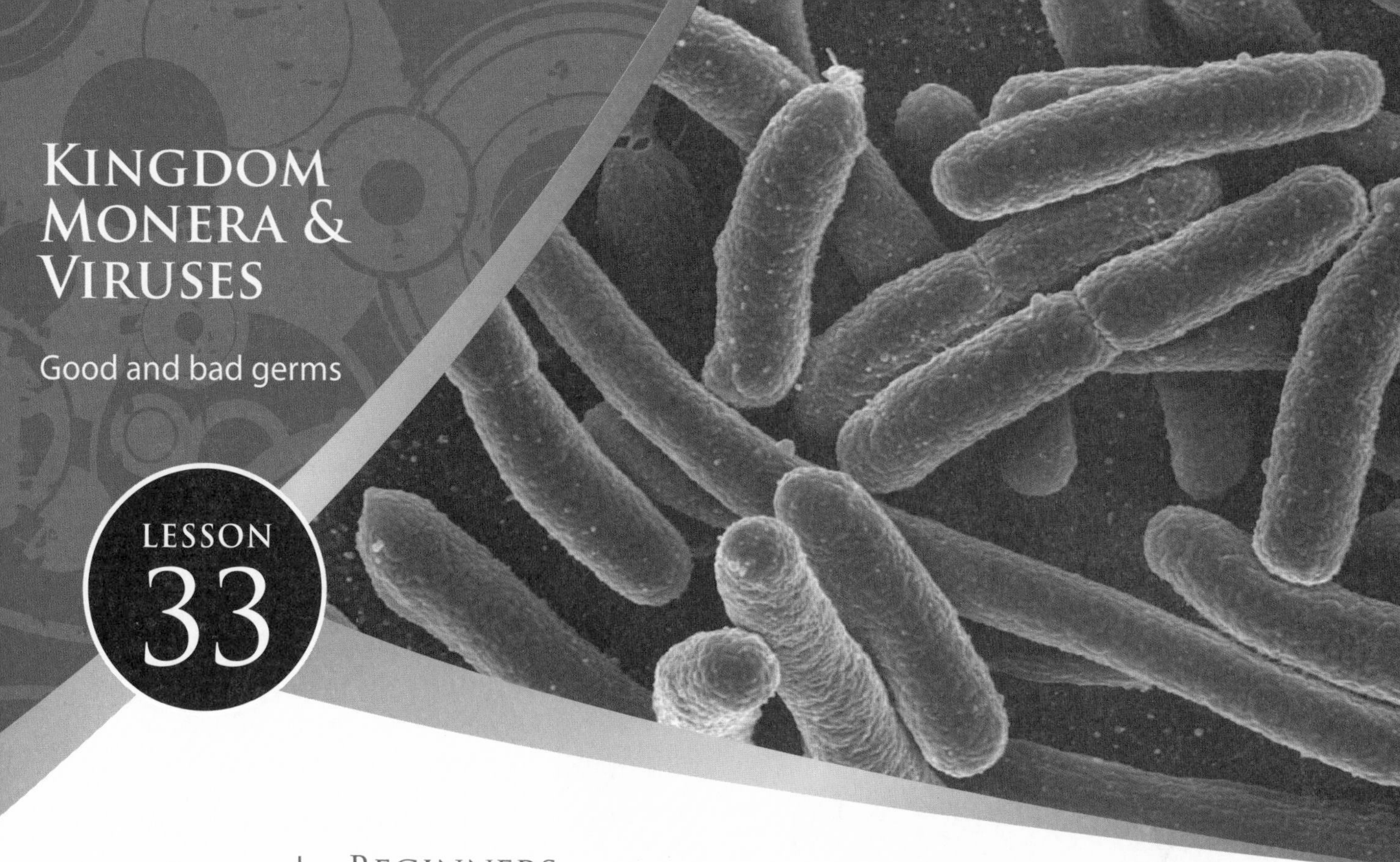

Kingdom Monera & Viruses

Good and bad germs

LESSON 33

How are bacteria and viruses different?

Words to know:

bacteria

moneran

virus

antibiotic

vaccine

Challenge words:

antibiotic resistant

Beginners

The last group of living creatures that you are going to learn about is **bacteria**. Bacteria are very small. They can only be seen with a microscope. **Viruses** are similar to bacteria in some ways but they are not living creatures. Viruses are so small they can only be seen with a very special microscope.

Many times bacteria and viruses are called germs. Germs can make you sick. Some germs can give you diseases such as chicken pox, measles, or a cold. However, not all germs are bad. Some bacteria can be very helpful. Some bacteria eat dead plants and animals, which is very helpful. Also, some bacteria are in your intestines and help you digest your food. You should do things to keep from getting sick, like washing your hands. You shouldn't sneeze or cough on other people, so you don't spread the bad germs, but you can also be thankful for the helpful bacteria too.

- **What are two types of germs?**
- **How can bacteria be helpful?**

The final group of living organisms is the monerans. These creatures include some of the germs that make you sick as well as the organisms that help recycle minerals from dead plants and animals. These creatures fit into two groups: bacteria and viruses. Monerans are not classified as animals or plants—they make up their own kingdom.

Bacteria are single-celled creatures. However, they do not have a defined nucleus like protists do. Some bacteria can produce their own food while others feed off other cells or dead plants and animals. Some bacteria make humans sick. Bacteria can cause plague, pneumonia, and tuberculosis. But not all bacteria are harmful. Most bacteria are very helpful. Bacteria are vital in the breakdown of dead plants and animals. Also, bacteria are necessary in the human digestive system. Without bacteria, our bodies cannot properly digest the food we eat.

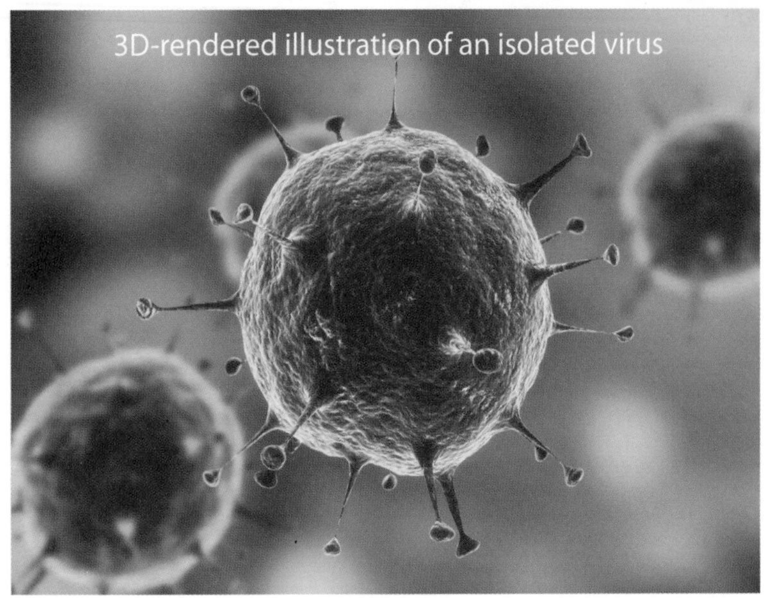
3D-rendered illustration of an isolated virus

Viruses are some of the smallest "creatures," yet they present some of the biggest puzzles to scientists. Scientists do not consider viruses as living things. A virus has genetic information like a cell but it does not directly reproduce. Instead, it invades a host cell and reprograms it to reproduce more viruses. Many of the diseases we are familiar with are caused by viruses, including flu, the common cold, chicken pox, and measles.

Scientists have discovered antibiotics, which are substances that can be used in the treatment of bacteria-induced diseases. However, few treatments have been found to cure diseases caused by viruses. Many of the more serious diseases can be prevented by the use of vaccines, which are substances that encourage your body to build up defenses against certain viruses but cannot cure the diseases. ■

Anti-Bacterial Hunt

Many of the items in our homes are anti-bacterial—that is, they kill bacteria. Search your house looking at things like hand soap, laundry soap, and cleaning supplies to see how many of them say "anti-bacterial" on them. Also, check medical supplies such as anti-bacterial creams or sprays, bandages, etc. People have become concerned about germs and want products that get rid of them in hopes of staying healthier.

WHAT DID WE LEARN?

- How are bacteria similar to plants and animals?
- How are bacteria different from plant and animal cells?
- How are viruses similar to plants and animals?
- How are viruses different?

TAKING IT FURTHER

- Answer the following questions to test if a virus is alive:

  Does it have cells? Can it reproduce? Is it growing? Does it move or respond to its environment? Does it need food and water? Does it have respiration? Is it alive?
- How can use of antibiotics be bad?

ANTIBIOTIC RESISTANCE

Antibiotics are very important in treating bacteria-induced diseases. However, scientists have seen a rise in **antibiotic resistant** strains of bacteria—bacteria that are not killed by a certain antibiotic like they have been in the past. Some scientists claim that this is a form of evolution and that the bacteria are evolving to fit their environment. But is this really true? Let's look at what is really happening.

Many bacteria, such as the bacteria that cause strep throat, can be killed with a drug called penicillin. Some of the strep bacteria are able to produce an enzyme called beta-lactamase. This enzyme breaks down the penicillin, which makes it harmless to the bacteria.

When a person takes penicillin, the bacteria that do not produce the enzyme will be killed first and the ones that do produce it will survive and reproduce. The bacteria in the next generation are more likely to be able to produce the enzyme and thus are more likely to survive and reproduce again. Eventually, enough of the bacteria can produce the enzyme that the patient does not get well and a different antibiotic must be used. Thus the bacteria are now said to be resistant to penicillin. But is this evolution?

Molecules-to-man evolution requires that new information be added to the DNA of the next generation. The bacteria did not acquire a new ability. They already had the ability to form the enzyme. So there is no new genetic information added and no evolution has taken place. It is survival of the fittest, but not evolution. This is no different than the faster deer being able to survive longer than the slower deer that are more likely to be eaten by predators. In fact, bacteria actually provide great evidence against evolution. Because bacteria reproduce very quickly we see many generations of bacteria in only a few days. In thousands of years bacteria go through millions of generations. There is a chance for changes to occur in the DNA of a creature each time it reproduces, so if changes in DNA cause evolution to occur, as the evolutionists claim, we should see the greatest changes in bacteria since they have gone through more generations than nearly any other living creature. However, when we compare fossilized bacteria to today's bacteria, there are very few differences, showing that even after millions of generations, no evolution has occurred. Even the smallest creatures support what the Bible says.

Louis Pasteur
Got Milk?

1822–1895

If you've got milk in your refrigerator, you might want to thank a French chemist named Louis Pasteur who was born two days after Christmas in 1822. His father had served in Napoleon's army and afterward worked as a tanner.

Louis Pasteur did a lot of work that we are still thankful for today, like what he did for milk. He came up with a way of processing the milk to kill off the bacteria so it will stay good for more than a couple of days. The process was named after him. We call it pasteurization. Look on your milk container to see if it says pasteurized on it.

He helped us in many other ways, too. Today, a woman can go to the hospital to deliver a baby and is able to enjoy the gift of a new life coming into the world without the fear of dying from infection. In Louis Pasteur's day, about one-third of the pregnant women in Paris died from childbirth fever or infection. Pasteur convinced the medical community that their sloppy practices were spreading germs and hurting their patients.

However, most of his ideas were not accepted easily. When he said doctors should wash their hands and sterilize their instruments, he really upset the medical community. He was called a menace to science. They said, "Who does Pasteur think that he is? He isn't even a medical doctor . . . just a lowly chemist."

The wife of the emperor asked Dr. Pasteur to come explain his radical views to the French Court. He told the emperor that the hospitals in Paris were death houses and that most of the doctors carried death on their hands (referring to germs). Even when he accurately predicted the death of the emperor's sister-in-law, he was condemned as a fraud and banned by the emperor from speaking out in public about medicine.

After this, Pasteur moved to the countryside where he spent the next ten years working to discover the causes of anthrax, the black plague of sheep. Anthrax had been ravaging the sheep across France. Pasteur invented an anthrax vaccine, which he gave to the farmers to use on their sheep for free.

At this time, the French government needed more sheep to pay the 5 million francs they owed to Germany for their war indemnity. They came to the area where Pasteur had been working with the farmers to find out why their sheep were so healthy. When Pasteur told them of his vaccine, he was again mocked as a fool by the Academy of Medicine. He showed them the truth by taking 50 sheep and vaccinating 25 of them. Then all 50 were infected with blood carrying anthrax. To everyone's amazement, only the sheep that had been vaccinated survived. Because of Pasteur's work, we now have a reliable cure for anthrax for both livestock and humans.

Even with this wonderful success, the medical establishment was slow to accept Pasteur. However, after nearly 40 years of work, he was elected as a member of the Académie Française in 1882. There he undertook the task of finding a cure for rabies. Three years later he was able to save the life of a young boy named Joseph Meister who had been bitten by a rabid dog. The boy survived and later become the caretaker of Pasteur's tomb at the world-famous Pasteur Institute in Paris. Louis Pasteur headed work at the Pasteur Institute, which was inaugurated in Paris in 1888, until his death on September 28, 1895.

Dr. Pasteur's work has saved millions of lives, but his discoveries came too late to save three of his daughters, who died from typhoid fever. Pasteur selflessly taught that the benefits of science are for all of humanity, not for the benefit of the scientist, and today all of humanity is reaping the benefits of his work.

Animal Notebook: Final Project

Putting the animals together

LESSON 34

What have you learned about animals?

After learning about many of the different creatures that God created, we can see that He created a wonderful world of life. From the most complex vertebrate to the single-celled protist, we can see the hand of the Master Designer. You have been making a notebook with all of your projects from this book. Now take what you have learned and finish up your book so you can share the world of animals with someone else. ■

Animal Notebook

As you have been studying the world of animals, you have been building a notebook. Below are some ideas for completing the notebook. You can make this as simple or complex as you desire.

It will be very beneficial to have library books available to provide additional information and ideas for the pages of your notebook.

It will probably take several days to complete this book. When you are done, you will have something that you can be proud of.

Some ideas for making pages in your notebook:

- Older children can write a report for each section of the book.
- If using a computer, add clip-art to your pages. Many pictures of animals are available in clip-art files.
- Be creative; don't make every section look like every other section.
- Clip pictures from old magazines or coloring books to add to your book.
- If you are artistic, you can draw pictures of many animals.

- Take photographs of projects you have completed in previous lessons and include them in your notebook.
- Add photographs of field trips you have taken.
- Include the worksheets you completed in previous lessons.
- Make a colorful title page.
- Make a table of contents; this will allow readers to find information quickly.

Vertebrates Section:

This should include information for all five types of vertebrates.

1. Mammals
2. Birds
3. Fish
4. Amphibians
5. Reptiles

Invertebrates Section:

This should include information for all six types of invertebrates.

1. Arthropods
2. Mollusks
3. Cnidarians
4. Echinoderms
5. Sponges
6. Worms

Protists and Monerans Section:

Even though they do not belong in the animal kingdom, include information for these interesting creatures.

1. Flagellates
2. Sarcodines (pseudopods)
3. Ciliates
4. Algae
5. Bacteria
6. Viruses

WHAT DID WE LEARN?

- What do all animals have in common?
- What is the difference between vertebrates and invertebrates?
- What sets protists apart from animals?

TAKING IT FURTHER

- What are some of the greatest or most interesting things you learned from your study of the world of animals?
- What would you like to learn more about?
- Read Genesis 1 and 2. Discuss what was created on each day and how each part completes the whole.

Conclusion

Reflecting on the world of animals

LESSON 35

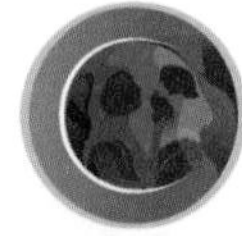

Thank God for animals.

We have studied the world of animals with its tremendous variety of creatures. As we think about the world of animals around us, we should be thankful to God for making such a wonderful world and giving us such variety. Take a few minutes and contemplate how glorious God's creation is. When God rested on the seventh day, it was indeed very good. And even though God's perfect creation has been corrupted by sin, He still wants us to study it, enjoy it, and take care of it.

Read Job 38:39–40:5 and discuss all the wonders mentioned in this passage. Discuss Job's response to God's questions. How should we respond to God's creation?

Use a Bible concordance or Bible encyclopedia and see how many different animals you can find mentioned in the Bible.

Now write a poem or prayer of thanksgiving to God for the amazing world of animals. ■

Glossary

Abdomen Back segment of an insect or other arthropod body

Airfoil Shape that causes air to flow faster over a surface than under it creating lift

Amphibian Animal that begins life breathing water and changes to be able to breathe air

Anal fin Fin on the underside near the back of the fish

Antibiotic Substance used to treat bacterial diseases

Apes Primates without tails including chimps and gorillas

Arachnid Animal with two body parts and eight legs

Arthropod Animal with segmented legs or feet

Bacteria Single-celled creatures without a defined nucleus

Baleen Comb-like structures in a whale's mouth for straining food

Binocular vision Eyes on the front of the head—each eye produces a slightly different view which when combined provides depth perception

Bivalve Mollusk with two-part shell

Blowhole Hole on the top of the head through which an aquatic mammal breathes

Cartilage Flexible material replacing bone in some fish

Caudal fin Tail fin

Cell membrane Outer covering of cell, acts like skin

Centipede Animal with segmented body with one pair of feet per segment

Cephalopod Mollusk with a merged head and foot and often no outer shell

Cephalothorax Body part that is a combined head and thorax

Chitin Starchy substance forming the exoskeleton

Chrysalis/Pupa The stage in which the larva turns into an adult

Ciliate Protist that moves using cilia

Cilia Tiny hairs that cover a surface

Cloaca Part of a bird's digestive system that releases waste

Cnidarians Animals with hollow bodies and stinging tentacles

Cold-blooded Animal that does not maintain a constant body temperature

Colubrid Most common group of snakes

Complete metamorphosis Change occurring in insects that look very different from their parents when they hatch

Compost Decomposed material, fertilizer

Concertina movement Moving by coiling and uncoiling

Constrictor Snake that kills its prey by squeezing

Contour feathers Feathers that cover a bird's body

Coral colony A collection of thousands of coral connected together

Coral reef A large collection of thousands of coral colonies connected together

Coral Tiny cnidarians that grow a crusty shell around their bodies

Crop Sac that releases food continuously into the bird's stomach

Crustacean Animal that has two body parts and crusty exoskeleton

Cytoplasm Liquid that fills a cell

Dorsal fins Fins on the top of the fish
Down feathers Fuzzy feathers providing insulation

Echinoderm Sea creature with spiny skin, often has five legs
Endoskeleton Internal skeleton
Esophagus Tube between the mouth and stomach
Exoskeleton Outer covering providing protection and support

Flagellate Protist that moves using a flagellum
Flagellum Whip-like structure that moves like a motor
Flatworm Non-segmented worms with flat bodies
Flight feathers Feathers that cover a bird's wings
Fluke Tail fin on an aquatic mammal

Gastropod Mollusk with one-part shell
Gills Organs for removing oxygen from water
Gizzard Rough organ to grind bird's food
Gullet Opening that serves as a mouth

Head Front segment of the insect body

Hibernation A type of extended period of sleep

Incomplete metamorphosis Change occurring in insects that look like their parents when they hatch
Insect Animal with three body parts, six legs, wings, and antennae
Invertebrate Animal without a backbone

Jacobson's organ Special organ for smell found in snakes and some other reptiles
Joey Immature marsupial

Keratin Material that forms hair, fingernails, and baleen

Larva/Larval stage Early stage of an animal that undergoes metamorphosis
Lateral undulation Moving in sideways waves

Mammal Warm-blooded animal with fur and mammary glands
Mammary glands Glands that secrete milk for feeding young
Mantle Organ that secretes a substance that forms a shell
Marsupial Mammal with a pouch for carrying developing young
Medusa Adult stage of a jellyfish's life cycle when it has a bell shaped body
Metamorphosis A significant change in form
Millipede Animal with segmented body with two pairs of feet per segment
Mitochondria Cell's power plants
Mollusk Soft bodied invertebrate with a muscular foot and usually a shell
Moneran Micro-organisms without a nucleus, including different bacteria
Myriapod Animal with many feet, specifically centipedes and millipedes

New World monkey Monkeys that live in the western hemisphere, have a prehensile tail
Nictitating membrane Clear eyelids that protect a reptile's eyes
Nocturnal Active at night
Nucleus Control center of the cell
Nymph Immature insect that experiences incomplete metamorphosis

Old World monkey Monkeys that live in the eastern hemisphere, do not have a prehensile tail

Parasite Animals that take nutrients from a living host
Pectoral fins Front fins used for angling up and down
Pelvic fins Fins on bottom of fish in center of body
Planula Worm-like stage in a jellyfish's life cycle before it becomes a polyp
Polyp The stage in a cnidarians life when it has hollow body with tentacles
Pore Small openings or holes
Preening Running the feather through the beak to re-hook the barbs
Prehensile tail One which has the ability to grasp

Primate Mammal with five fingers, five toes, and binocular vision

Protist A diverse group of simple creatures with a nucleus

Pseudopod Foot or finger-like projection of a cell

Rectilinear movement Moving by contracting and stretching to move in a straight line

Regenerate To regrow a lost body part

Rostrum Beak of a dolphin

Roundworm Non-segmented worms with round bodies

Sarcodine Protist that moves using pseudopods

Scavengers Animals that eat dead plants or animals

Segmented body Animal with distinct sections of its body

Segmented worm Worm with rings or segments to its body

Side winding Moving forward at an angle by moving sideways at the same time

Spinnerets Organs which produce silky thread

Sponge Simple animal with many pores

Swim bladder Balloon-like sac used for buoyancy

Symbiotic relationship Two or more creatures living in a mutually beneficial way

Tadpole/Pollywog The larva or infant form of an amphibian

Talons Claw-like feet

Thorax Middle segment of the insect body

Vaccine Substance that causes a body to build immunity to disease

Vacuole Storage area in a cell

Venomous Snakes that have a poisonous bite

Vertebrae Small bones that protect the spinal cord

Vertebrate Animal with a backbone

Virus Sub-microscopic agent that causes disease

Warm-blooded Animal that maintains a constant body temperature

Challenge Glossary

Abomasum Fourth chamber of a ruminant's stomach

Antibiotic resistant bacteria Bacteria that are not killed by certain antibiotics

Bioluminescence Process producing light in an animal through chemical reactions

Biomimetics Study of living creatures for human technology

Buoyant Able to float

Carapace Top part of a turtle shell

Casque Large bony structure on the head of a cassowary bird

Ceratopsians Horned dinosaurs

Chemosynthesis Process of converting chemicals into food

Circular canal Central canal pumping water to the ray canals

Compound eye Eye with multiple lenses

Counter-current exchange Air and blood flow in opposite directions through the lungs

Cud The food that is regurgitated for more chewing

Digitigrade Walking on the base or flats of the toes

Echolocation Sonar used by animals for communication

Fiber optics Use of tiny glass tubes to transmit light

Hemoglobin Substance that turns bright red in the presence of oxygen

Hydrothermal vent Area on ocean floor where super-heated water flows out

Lateral line Series of nerves covering the head and sides of a fish

Olfactory lobe Part of the brain responsible for the sense of smell

Omasum Third chamber of a ruminant's stomach

Open circulatory system One with no blood vessels to carry the blood

Optic lobe Part of the brain responsible for the sense of sight

Plantigrade Walking on the soles of the feet

Plasmodium Sporozoan that causes malaria

Plastron Bottom part of a turtle shell

Plated dinosaurs Dinosaurs with large plates along their backs

Plume End of a tubeworm's body

Ray canals Tubes carrying water to the rays of the starfish

Reticulum Second chamber of a ruminant's stomach

Rorqual Whales with grooved expandable throats

Rumen First chamber of a ruminant's four chambered stomach

Ruminant Animal that regurgitates and rechews its food

Sauropods Large dinosaurs with long necks and tails

Sieve plate Openings through which water enters the water vascular system

Siphonophore A colony of cnidarians living together to form one organism

Spiracles Openings in an insect's side for air flow

Sporozoan Protist that produces spores

Stance The way an animal walks on its feet

Theropods Meat eating dinosaurs

Tube feet Rows of tubes on the underside of each starfish ray

Tube worm Worm that thrives near hydrothermal vents

Ungulates Animals with an unguligrade stance

Unguligrade Walking on the tips of the toes, usually with hooves

Urticating hairs Barbed hairs on a spider that produce irritation in enemies

Water vascular system Series of tubes that carry water throughout the starfish's body

Index

1:1
answersingenesis.org
believing it. defending it. proclaiming it.